Barnes & Noble Shakespeare

David Scott Kastan
Series Editor

BARNES & NOBLE SHAKESPEARE features newly edited texts of the plays prepared by the world's premiere Shakespeare scholars. Each edition provides new scholarship with an introduction, commentary, unusually full and informative notes, an account of the play as it would have been performed in Shakespeare's theaters, and an essay on how to read Shakespeare's language.

DAVID SCOTT KASTAN is the Old Dominion Foundation Professor in the Humanities at Columbia University and one of the world's leading authorities on Shakespeare.

Barnes & Noble Shakespeare
Published by Barnes & Noble
122 Fifth Avenue
New York, NY 10011
www.barnesandnoble.com/shakespeare

Image on p. 276:
By Permission of the Folger Shakespeare Library.

Library of Congress Cataloging-in-Publication Data

Shakespeare, William, 1564–1616.
  Merchant of Venice / William Shakespeare.
    p. cm. — (Barnes and Noble Shakespeare)
  Includes bibliographical references.
  ISBN-13: 978-1-4114-0085-6
  ISBN-10: 1-4114-0085-2
  1. Shylock (Fictitious character)—Drama. 2. Jews—Italy—Drama. 3. Venice (Italy)—Drama. 4. Moneylenders—Drama. I. Title.

  PR2825.A1 2006
  822.3'3—dc22
                    2006018628

Printed and bound in the United States
      7 9 10 8

THE
MERCHANT OF VENICE

William
SHAKESPEARE

JULIE CRAWFORD
EDITOR

Barnes & Noble Shakespeare

Contents

Introduction to *The Merchant of Venice* 1

Shakespeare and His England 11

William Shakespeare: A Chronology 21

Words, Words, Words: Understanding Shakespeare's

    Language 25

Key to the Play Text 37

The Merchant of Venice 39

    List of Roles 41

    Act 1 43

    Act 2 85

    Act 3 149

    Act 4 205

    Act 5 249

Editing *The Merchant of Venice* 277

The Merchant of Venice on the Early Stage 283

Significant Performances 291

Inspired by *The Merchant of Venice* 295

For Further Reading 303

Introduction to *The Merchant of Venice*
by Julie Crawford

I n the climactic scene of *The Merchant of Venice*, the character Portia, cross-dressed and disguised as a male legal scholar, enters a courtroom in which Antonio, the merchant of the play's title, confronts Shylock the Jew. "Which is the merchant here, and which the Jew?" she asks. After three acts in which the characters have taken great pains to insist on the utter difference between Antonio and Shylock, indeed between Shylock and all of the Christian characters, Portia's apparent inability to tell the difference between them strikes us as odd—a not very promising beginning to her courtroom career. Yet the fact that it is Portia who calls upon the two to distinguish themselves and be judged demonstrates her central role in this play. Both a rich heiress and a "learnèd doctor," Portia is at once a desirable commodity and an active agent. She is the bridge between the aristocratic and romantic world of Belmont in which people "hazard," or risk, everything for love, and the mercantile world of Venice in which people risk everything for profit. She is also the bridge between the world of marriage and the world of powerful relations between men. Indeed once Portia's use of the law cuts Shylock from the plot, it is her ring that brings the different aspects of the plot together: Venice and Belmont, merchants and aristocrats, men and women.

Nonetheless, the character who has drawn the most attention and fascination from audiences is Shylock—indeed, the play was also known in Shakespeare's time as *The Jew of Venice*. Shylock is the great enigma at the heart of the play. Some have seen his story as a tragedy, making *The Merchant of Venice*, in W.H. Auden's words, one of Shakespeare's "Unpleasant Plays," while others have seen him as the villain of a comedy who must be excised to bring about a happy ending. The Christian characters' harsh treatment of Shylock may reflect the way Elizabethans saw Jews (who had been officially banished from England in 1290) and usurers—those who lend money at excessive rates of interest. Alternately, their treatment of Shylock may be meant to highlight the hypocrisy of the Christians who spit on Jews and, as Shylock points out, own slaves, a practice that, like usury, earns money for people through no labor of their own. Many Christians believed that the conversion of the Jews was the end goal of Christianity, but they were also what we would call anti-Semitic, believing, as the seventeenth-century writer Thomas Calvert put it, that Jews "have a bloody thirst after the blood of Christians."

Shylock is repeatedly referred to as a "devil" by the other characters, and Shakespeare's audience may have seen him as a descendant of the familiar figure of Vice from medieval morality plays, an exaggerated, stylized villain who shares his schemes with the audience in comical asides. Apart from the mere fact of his being a Jew, the controversial thing he does, for which the Christian characters censure and demonize him, is practice usury. Usury, the business of lending money at (often extreme) interest rates, was widely criticized in the period in such tracts as Miles Mosse's *The Arraignment and Conviction of Usury* (1595). Whether this practice alone would have definitively established Shylock as an evil character for Shakespeare's audience is open to question, however. Usury was in fact widely practiced in England, as evidenced by the fact that Queen Elizabeth officially set the rate of interest on loans at 10 percent.

Indeed, Shakespeare's company, the Lord Chamberlain's Men, built its theaters on money borrowed at interest, and Shakespeare himself loaned money at high interest rates and took people to court when they failed to repay him. The Venetian state relied on a community of Jews for a wide range of financial services, including the providing of loans, but usury, as it was for England, was certainly part of that city-state's busy and complex economy. It is worthwhile to point out that it is others who call what Shylock does "usury"; he himself calls it "well-won thrift" (1.3.46). In fact, we never do see him practicing usury in the course of the play; he refuses to charge Antonio interest on his loan, insisting instead on the famous bond of a pound of flesh, something that, as Shylock points out, is worth less than a pound of beef.

According to Shylock, Antonio is the problem in Venice. Shylock hates him not only because he's a Christian, but because he lends money for free and thus brings down the rate of usury. While the battle between the two men is religious—as Shylock points out, Antonio "hates our sacred nation" (1.3.44)—it is also economic. Shylock wants Antonio gone so he can make money; Antonio, it turns out, not only refuses to lend or borrow by taking or giving excess, but he has also often helped those that have come to him after forfeiting on Shylock's loans. These choices are given clear moral weight in the play: Shylock is selfish with his money, and Antonio is generous; Shylock hoards his ducats whereas Antonio opens up his purse for others. Yet the moral weight is not all on one side. Shylock's desire for revenge is based, among other things, on Antonio's spitting hatred: as Shylock says following his famous speech about Jewish humanity, he learned his "villainy" from his persecutors. Shylock's desire for Antonio's pound of flesh certainly picks up on anti-Semitic histories and beliefs (particularly the association between Jews and cannibalism), but he is nonetheless far more than an unmitigated villain. While others romanticize Antonio's economic enterprises—Salerio imagines Antonio's ships as if they were "pageants of the sea" (1.1.11)—Shylock is refreshingly straightforward about them: "ships are but boards," he tells Bassanio, "sailors but men" (1.3.20). When his daughter Jessica literally tosses his money from his house and exchanges his wife's ring for a monkey, we feel Shylock's losses even as we condemn his increasing cruelty to Antonio.

Antonio's own status as a moral arbiter is somewhat questionable. First, he is not nearly as financially stable as he claims to be when he tells Salerio and Solanio at the beginning of the play that his "ventures are not in one bottom trusted, / Nor to one place, nor is my whole estate / Upon the fortune of this present year" (1.1.42–44). We find out shortly that in fact all his fortunes *are* at sea and he has neither "money nor commodity / To raise a present sum" (178–179) for his friend Bassanio. He thus tells Bassanio to try his credit in Venice, taking the two men, and the plot, to Shylock. Antonio turns very quickly to a practice he condemns, suggesting if not hypocrisy (what does it mean to use a service to which you claim to be ethically opposed?) at least a more complicated financial profile than the one he initially presents. We learn after the (reputed) loss of his ships that Antonio's "creditors" are growing cruel and thus that there are others besides Shylock who have loaned him money. Such credit was an integral part of venturing or hazarding for profit and was thus considered a separate economic activity from usury, the unnatural "breeding" of money through interest. But Antonio nonetheless shares an economic vocabulary with Shylock. At the end of the trial scene, Antonio asks to have half of Shylock's money "in use to render it / Upon his death" to Lorenzo and Jessica (4.1.380–381). He does not say that he is going to keep Shylock's money locked in a casket for safekeeping; he is going to use it to make money. It is hard to forget that Shylock decries the fact that Antonio hates him "for use of that which is mine own" (1.3.109). They are both *using* money to make money, in other words, one way is just more acceptable than the other. Both the merchant and the Jew are engaged in similarly risky and potentially lucrative enterprises.

Bassanio himself seems to be a risky financial enterprise. When we first meet him, he refers to his great debts and disabled estate and admits to showing a more "swelling port" than he can afford. Indeed his first question in the play, "when shall we laugh?" suggests that he is, for the most part, happily oblivious to the harsher facts of life. Antonio's immediate offer of his purse, person, and "extremest means" to his friend thus seems like something of a bad economic decision. When Bassanio later gives his new servant Launcelot a highly decorated uniform and invites his entire "acquaintance" to an elaborate feast, we are aware both that these outlays are signs of a "swelling port" and that they are being funded by Antonio. Yet like Antonio and Shylock, Bassanio has a financial plan. Bassanio's pursuit of Portia, whom he first describes as a "lady richly left" (1.1.161), is an economic venture fraught, much like Antonio's ventures at sea, with both competition and risk. Had he the financial means to compete with Portia's other suitors, he tells Antonio, "I have a mind presages me such thrift / That I should questionless be fortunate" (1.1.175–176). It is only later that Bassanio talks about his pursuit of Portia in romantic and heroic terms—like Jason pursuing the "golden fleece"—and by that point we are well aware of the extent to which Antonio's purse and person are at risk in the venture. When Antonio tells Bassanio that his credit will be "racked even to the uttermost" (1.1.181) to support his friend, he not only foreshadows his future suffering and trial but signals the extremes to which he will go to serve Bassanio. Antonio's first words in the play express an inexplicable sadness, and we later hear that he weeps when saying good-bye to Bassanio on precisely the venture he has "racked" himself to fund. Bassanio, in other words, is a risk Antonio is willing to take.

Bassanio and Antonio are tied together in a complex bond of risk in the play, but they are also tied together by an intense bond of "amity," a term for male friendship that encompasses a wide range of feelings and loyalties. Antonio "only loves the world" for

Bassanio (2.8.50), and Bassanio claims in Act Four that he would choose Bassanio over his wife. Most contemporary editions of the play anxiously explain that the terms Bassanio and Antonio use for one another, including "bosom lover," could simply be synonyms for "good friend" in the period. Yet both "lover" and "friend" can mean different things at different points in history, and if the modern conception of "homosexual" did not exist in the early seventeenth century, neither did modern homophobia. The relationship between the men was undoubtedly as profound as the terms and vows used to describe it—what Salerio calls an "affection wondrous sensible" (2.8.48). It is this bond with Bassanio that makes Antonio bind himself to Shylock; he ventures for love in this case, not profit, and in many ways this is the value the play most explicitly upholds.

When we first meet Portia she is, like Antonio, both melancholic and unhappy with her own situation. She is also, again like Antonio, engaged in an elaborate game of risk. (Portia herself calls it the "lottery" of her destiny.) While Portia's risk concerns caskets and marital anxiety rather than argosies and "racked" credit, the stakes are similarly high: Both her inheritance and her marital future hang in the balance. Much like Helen standing on the walls of Troy and evaluating the soldiers who have come to fight, Portia makes observations about the men who come to Belmont to venture for her hand, dispensing judgments about ethnicity (the English, for example, have no independent identity of their own) and "complexion." While the trade and profit of Venice is made up of "all nations" and Antonio's argosies venture as far as Tripoli, Barbary, and Mexico, so do ships from all over the world come bearing their Jasons to Belmont. Portia's judgment of her suitors thus outlines some of the play's values—"all nations" are not equally desirable—but it also signals her capacity for the (literally) discriminating judgment that will be shown to full advantage in the trial scene.

Bassanio makes his bid for Portia's hand right after we learn that one of Antonio's ships has wrecked in the Goodwins. After rejecting the gold and silver caskets, which represent the deceptiveness of ornament and the tedium of everyday commerce, Bassanio chooses the lead casket. In many ways, his choice signals the triumph of the economic and emotional values of the play: as the casket's message announces, "Who chooseth me must give and hazard all he hath" (2.7.9). Despite the lost ship, then, hazarding is validated—Bassanio's choice is clearly the _right_ choice; it wins him Portia's hand and estate. (As the Prince of Morocco notes earlier in the play, "Men that hazard all / Do it in hope of fair advantages" [2.7.18–19].) Indeed immediately after Bassanio makes his choice the fair advantages seem to multiply. The newly won Portia wishes she would be "trebled twenty times" herself to stand high in Bassanio's account (3.2.153). Her statement that she is "an unlessoned girl, unschooled, unpracticed" (3.2.159) is both an accounting (to her, this sum is negligible) and a foreshadowing of her future turn as a learned doctor. Yet as it turns out it is not her money that saves Antonio but something equally valuable: her intelligence.

When Portia offers everything she has to Bassanio, making him, at least in the heat of the moment, "her lord, her governor, her king" (3.2.165), she also makes a deal. The house, the servants, and myself are yours, she tells Bassanio,

> I give them with this ring,
> Which when you part from, lose, or give away,
> Let it presage the ruin of your love
> And be my vantage to exclaim on you. (3.2.171–174)

If Bassanio loses her ring, in other words, Portia will have "vantage" over him. "Vantage," or "advantage," means superiority in a contest, but it also means profit or interest. Like everyone else in the play, that is, Portia is taking a risk that may well bring her more than her initial investment. (And, as we shall see, it does; when the ring comes back it brings not only Bassanio but Antonio as well.)

Before Portia gains any advantage, the news comes about Antonio's misfortunes, and Portia must leave Belmont for Venice. The "unlessoned girl" must become the "learnèd doctor" Balthazar, the world of landed and inherited property must interact with the world of merchants, and Antonio must be freed from his bond with Shylock to free Bassanio for her. It is here that the play turns its attention from its validation of risk and love to a concern with justice and mercy. The trial scene is both intensely dramatic and heavily symbolic. Shylock stands for Old Testament justice, or what he calls "law," and Portia/Balthazar for Christian mercy, expressed in terms both biblically poetic ("The quality of mercy is not strained" [182]) and candid (as Portia points out, if justice really existed, none of us would be saved). But the trial scene is also specifically concerned with *Venetian* justice. With the brief and notable exception of Bassanio, who wants to selfishly wrest it to serve his own purposes, everyone in the play upholds the law of Venice, a city whose traffic, as we have seen, "Consisteth of all nations." And yet when Portia/Balthazar takes recourse to the *other* law—the one that punishes "aliens"—we cannot help but notice that Venetian law does *not* serve all nations equally. The mercy Antonio eventually offers to Shylock may work in a Christian register—Christians believed baptism would save the Jews from damnation—but it is also cruel, predicated as it is on taking from Shylock his livelihood as well as his religion. The quality of mercy in the play is further tempered not only by Antonio's plans to make "use" of his money, but by Gratiano calling for the gallows as Shylock limps away.

It is not only Shylock and his money that are put to new use in Act Four—so is Bassanio. When Bassanio says that he would give everything, including his wife, to save Antonio, Portia/Balthazar is able to say, with considerable irony, that his wife would give him little thanks for the sentiment. This moment of dramatic irony fore-shadows the final act's disciplining of the "Christian husbands" who give away their rings. Antonio is, as he says after the trial, indebted in both love and service to Portia/Balthazar. Indeed he himself becomes the bond, or what Portia calls the "surety," for Bassanio's future loyalty to his wife in the play's final act. In this scene, Portia commands the grateful Antonio to give her ring back to Bassanio. "Here, Lord Bassanio."— Antonio says—"Swear to keep this ring" (5.1.256). While this scene has Antonio putting the ring on Bassanio's hand— representing yet another bond between the two men—he does so clearly in the service of Portia's "vantage."

The play's final bonding happens in its last act, when the couples are reconciled in Belmont. Act Five famously begins under the moonlight, with talk of love, and the sound of music; it is, at least at the outset, characterized by "sweet harmony" (5.1.57). Yet it is important to point out that Lorenzo and Jessica—an "unthrift love" if there ever was one—tell love stories that are stories of loss. In addition, the couples' reunion begins with a joke about infidelity ("a light wife doth make a heavy husband" [129]) and a quarrel. The "sweet harmony" of the final act is thus mitigated by a variety of factors. Portia brings male amity and merchant wealth into an alliance with marriage and landed wealth (it is in Belmont that the very-welcomed Antonio learns his ships have come in), but the risks one takes in marriage—the risk, among other things, that your partner will take an interest in someone else—are still alive and well. *The Merchant of Venice* may officially end in the romance of moonlight, but, as Portia puts it, "It is almost morning."

Shakespeare and His England
by David Scott Kastan

S hakespeare is a household name, one of those few that don't need a first name to be instantly recognized. His first name was, of course, William, and he (and it, in its Latin form, *Gulielmus*) first came to public notice on April 26, 1564, when his baptism was recorded in the parish church of Stratford-upon-Avon, a small market town about ninety miles northwest of London. It isn't known exactly when he was born, although traditionally his birthday is taken to be April 23rd. It is a convenient date (perhaps too convenient) because that was the date of his death in 1616, as well as the date of St. George's Day, the annual feast day of England's patron saint. It is possible Shakespeare was born on the 23rd; no doubt he was born within a day or two of that date. In a time of high rates of infant mortality, parents would not wait long after a baby's birth for the baptism. Twenty percent of all children would die before their first birthday.

Life in 1564, not just for infants, was conspicuously vulnerable. If one lived to age fifteen, one was likely to live into one's fifties, but probably no more than 60 percent of those born lived past their mid-teens. Whole towns could be ravaged by epidemic disease. In 1563, the year before Shakespeare was born, an outbreak of plague claimed over one third of the population of London. Fire, too, was a constant threat; the thatched roofs of many houses were highly flammable, as well as offering handy nesting places for insects and rats. Serious crop failures in several years of the decade of the 1560s created food shortages, severe enough in many cases to lead to the starvation of the elderly and the infirm, and lowering the resistances of many others so that between 1536 and 1560 influenza claimed over 200,000 lives.

Shakespeare's own family in many ways reflected these unsettling realities. He was one of eight children, two of whom did not survive their first year, one of whom died at age eight; one lived to twenty-seven, while the four surviving siblings died at ages ranging from Edmund's thirty-nine to William's own fifty-two years. William married at an unusually early age. He was only eighteen, though his wife was twenty-six, almost exactly the norm of the day for women, though men normally married also in their mid- to late twenties. Shakespeare's wife Anne was already pregnant at the time that the marriage was formally confirmed, and a daughter, Susanna, was born six months later, in May 1583. Two years later, she gave birth to twins, Hamnet and Judith. Hamnet would die in his eleventh year.

If life was always at risk from what Shakespeare would later call "the thousand natural shocks / That flesh is heir to" (*Hamlet*, 3.1.61–62), the incessant threats to peace were no less unnerving, if usually less immediately life threatening. There were almost daily rumors of foreign invasion and civil war as the Protestant Queen Elizabeth assumed the crown in 1558 upon the death of her Catholic half sister, Mary. Mary's reign had been marked by the public burnings of Protestant "heretics," by the seeming subordination of England to Spain, and by a commitment to a ruinous war with France, that, among its other effects, fueled inflation and encouraged a debasing of the currency. If, for many, Elizabeth represented the hopes for a peaceful and prosperous Protestant future, it seemed unlikely in the early days of her rule that the young monarch could hold her England together against the twin menace of the powerful Catholic monarchies of Europe and the significant part of her own population who were reluctant to give up their old faith. No wonder the Queen's principal secretary saw England in the early years of Elizabeth's rule as a land surrounded by "perils many, great and imminent."

In Stratford-upon-Avon, it might often have been easy to forget what threatened from without. The simple rural life, shared by about 90 percent of the English populace, had its reassuring natural rhythms and delights. Life was structured by the daily rising and setting of the sun, and by the change of seasons. Crops were planted and harvested; livestock was bred, its young delivered; sheep were sheared, some livestock slaughtered. Market days and fairs saw the produce and crafts of the town arrayed as people came to sell and shop—and be entertained by musicians, dancers, and troupes of actors. But even in Stratford, the lurking tensions and dangers could be daily sensed. A few months before Shakespeare was born, there had been a shocking "defacing" of images in the church, as workmen, not content merely to whitewash over the religious paintings decorating the interior as they were ordered, gouged large holes in those felt to be too "Catholic"; a few months after Shakespeare's birth, the register of the same church records another deadly outbreak of plague. The sleepy market town on the northern bank of the gently flowing river Avon was not immune from the menace of the world that surrounded it.

This was the world into which Shakespeare was born. England at his birth was still poor and backward, a fringe nation on the periphery of Europe. English itself was a minor language, hardly spoken outside of the country's borders. Religious tension was inescapable, as the old Catholic faith was trying determinedly to hold on, even as Protestantism was once again anxiously trying to establish itself as the national religion. The country knew itself vulnerable to serious threats both from without and from within. In 1562, the young Queen, upon whom so many people's hopes rested, almost fell victim to smallpox, and in 1569 a revolt of the Northern earls tried to remove her from power and restore Catholicism as the national religion. The following year, Pope

Pius V pronounced the excommunication of "Elizabeth, the pretended queen of England" and forbade Catholic subjects obedience to the monarch on pain of their own excommunication. "Now we are in an evil way and going to the devil," wrote one clergyman, "and have all nations in our necks."

It was a world of dearth, danger, and domestic unrest. Yet it would soon dramatically change, and Shakespeare's literary contribution would, for future generations, come to be seen as a significant measure of England's remarkable transformation. In the course of Shakespeare's life, England, hitherto an unsophisticated and under-developed backwater acting as a bit player in the momentous political dramas taking place on the European continent, became a confident, prosperous, global presence. But this new world was only accidentally, as it is often known today, "The Age of Shakespeare." To the degree that historical change rests in the hands of any individual, credit must be given to the Queen. This new world arguably was "The Age of Elizabeth," even if it was not the Elizabethan Golden Age, as it has often been portrayed.

The young Queen quickly imposed her personality upon the nation. She had talented councilors around her, all with strong ties to her of friendship or blood, but the direction of government was her own. She was strong willed and cautious, certain of her right to rule and convinced that stability was her greatest responsibility. The result may very well have been, as historians have often charged, that important issues facing England were never dealt with head-on and left to her successors to settle, but it meant also that she was able to keep her England unified and for the most part at peace.

Religion posed her greatest challenge, though it is important to keep in mind that in this period, as an official at Elizabeth's court said, "Religion and the commonwealth cannot be parted asunder." Faith then was not the largely voluntary commitment it is today, nor was there any idea of some separation of church and state. Religion was literally a matter of life and death, of salvation and damnation, and the Church was the Church of England. Obedience to it was not only a matter of conscience but also of law. It was the single issue on which the nation was most likely to be torn apart.

Elizabeth's great achievement was that she was successful in ensuring that the Church of England became formally a Protestant Church, but she did so without either driving most of her Catholic subjects to sedition or alienating the more radical Protestant community. The so-called "Elizabethan Settlement" forged a broad Christian community of what has been called prayer-book Protestantism, even as many of its practitioners retained, as a clergyman said, "still a smack and savor of popish principles." If there were forces on both sides who were uncomfortable with the Settlement—committed Protestants, who wanted to do away with all vestiges of the old faith, and convinced Catholics, who continued to swear their allegiance to Rome—the majority of the country, as she hoped, found ways to live comfortably both within the law and within their faith. In 1571, she wrote to the Duke of Anjou that the forms of worship she recommended would "not properly compel any man to alter his opinion in the great matters now in controversy in the Church." The official toleration of religious ambiguity, as well as the familiar experience of an official change of state religion accompanying the crowning of a new monarch, produced a world where the familiar labels of Protestant and Catholic failed to define the forms of faith that most English people practiced. But for Elizabeth, most matters of faith could be left to individuals, as long as the Church itself, and Elizabeth's position at its head, would remain unchallenged.

In international affairs, she was no less successful with her pragmatism and willingness to pursue limited goals. A complex mix of prudential concerns about religion, the economy, and national security drove her foreign policy. She did not have imperial ambitions; in the main, she wanted only to be sure there would be no invasion of England and to encourage English trade. In the event, both goals brought England into conflict with Spain, determining the increasingly anti-Catholic tendencies of English foreign policy and, almost accidentally, England's emergence as a world power. When Elizabeth came to the throne, England was in many ways a mere satellite nation to the Netherlands, which was part of the Hapsburg Empire that the Catholic Philip II (who had briefly and unhappily been married to her predecessor and half sister, Queen Mary) ruled from Spain; by the end of her reign England was Spain's most bitter rival.

The transformation of Spain from ally to enemy came in a series of small steps (or missteps), no one of which was intended to produce what in the end came to pass. A series of posturings and provocations on both sides led to the rupture. In 1568, things moved to their breaking point, as the English confiscated a large shipment of gold that the Spanish were sending to their troops in the Netherlands. The following year saw the revolt of the Catholic earls in Northern England, followed by the papal excommunication of the Queen in 1570, both of which were by many in England assumed to be at the initiative, or at very least with the tacit support, of Philip. In fact he was not involved, but England under Elizabeth would never again think of Spain as a loyal friend or reliable ally. Indeed, Spain quickly became its mortal enemy. Protestant Dutch rebels had been opposing the Spanish domination of the Netherlands since the early 1560s, but, other than periodic financial support, Elizabeth had done little to encourage them. But in 1585, she sent troops under the command of the Earl of Leicester to support the Dutch rebels against the Spanish. Philip decided then to launch a full-scale attack on England, with the aim of deposing Elizabeth and restoring the Catholic faith. An English assault on Cadiz in 1587 destroyed a number of Spanish ships, postponing Philip's plans, but in the summer of 1588 the mightiest navy in the world, Philip's grand armada, with 132 ships and 30,493 sailors and troops, sailed for England.

By all rights, it should have been a successful invasion, but a combination of questionable Spanish tactics and a fortunate shift of wind resulted in one of England's greatest victories. The English had twice failed to intercept the armada off the coast of Portugal, and the Spanish fleet made its way to England, almost catching the English ships resupplying in Plymouth. The English navy was on its heels, when conveniently the Spanish admiral decided to anchor in the English Channel off the French port of Calais to wait for additional troops coming from the Netherlands. The English attacked with fireships, sinking four Spanish galleons, and strong winds from the south prevented an effective counterattack from the Spanish. The Spanish fleet was pushed into the North Sea, where it regrouped and decided its safest course was to attempt the difficult voyage home around Scotland and Ireland, losing almost half its ships on the way. For many in England the improbable victory was a miracle, evidence of God's favor for Elizabeth and the Protestant nation. Though war with Spain would not end for another fifteen years, the victory over the armada turned England almost overnight into a major world power, buoyed by confidence that they were chosen by God and, more tangibly, by a navy that could compete for control of the seas.

From a backward and insignificant Hapsburg satellite, Elizabeth's England had become, almost by accident, the leader of Protestant Europe. But if the victory over the armada signaled England's new place in the world, it hardly marked the end of England's travails. The economy, which initially was fueled by the military buildup, in the early 1590s fell victim to inflation, heavy taxation to support the war with Spain, the inevitable wartime disruptions of trade, as well as crop failures and a general economic downturn in Europe. Ireland, over which England had been attempting to impose its rule since 1168, continued to be a source of trouble and great expense (in some years costing the crown nearly one fifth of its total revenues). Even when the most organized of the rebellions, begun in 1594 and led by Hugh O'Neill, Earl of Tyrone, formally ended in 1603, peace and stability had not been achieved.

But perhaps the greatest instability came from the uncertainty over the succession, an uncertainty that marked Elizabeth's reign from its beginning. Her near death from smallpox in 1562 reminded the nation that an unmarried queen could not insure the succession, and Elizabeth was under constant pressure to marry and produce an heir. She was always aware of and deeply resented the pressure, announcing as early as 1559: "this shall be for me sufficient that a marble stone shall declare that a queen, having reigned such a time, lived and died a virgin." If, however, it was for her "sufficient," it was not so for her advisors and for much of the nation, who hoped she would wed. Arguably Elizabeth was the wiser, knowing that her unmarried hand was a political advantage, allowing her to diffuse threats or create alliances with the seeming possibility of a match. But as with so much in her reign, the strategy bought temporary stability at the price of longer-term solutions.

By the mid 1590s, it was clear that she would die unmarried and without an heir, and various candidates were positioning themselves to succeed her. Enough anxiety was produced that all published debate about the succession was forbidden by law. There was no direct descendant of the English crown to claim rule, and all the claimants had to reach well back into their family history to find some legitimacy. The best genealogical claim belonged to King James VI of Scotland. His mother, Mary, Queen of Scots, was the granddaughter of James IV of Scotland and Margaret Tudor, sister to Elizabeth's father, Henry VIII. Though James had right on his side, he was, it must be remembered, a foreigner. Scotland shared the island with England but was a separate nation. Great Britain, the union of England and Scotland, would not exist formally until 1707, but with Elizabeth's death early in the morning of March 24, 1603, surprisingly uneventfully the thirty-seven-year-old James succeeded to the English throne. Two nations, one king: King James VI of Scotland, King James I of England.

Most of his English subjects initially greeted the announcement of their new monarch with delight, relieved that the crown had successfully been transferred without any major disruption and reassured that the new King was married with two living sons. However, quickly many became disenchanted with a foreign King who spoke English with a heavy accent, and dismayed even further by the influx of Scots in positions of power. Nonetheless, the new King's greatest political liability may well have been less a matter of nationality than of temperament: he had none of Elizabeth's skill and ease in publicly wooing her subjects. The Venetian ambassador wrote back to the doge that the new King was unwilling to "caress the people, nor make them that good cheer the late Queen did, whereby she won their loves."

He was aloof and largely uninterested in the daily activities of governing, but he was interested in political theory and strongly committed to the cause of peace. Although a steadfast Protestant, he lacked the reflexive anti-Catholicism of many of his subjects. In England, he achieved a broadly consensual community of Protestants. The so-called King James Bible, the famous translation published first in 1611, was the result of a widespread desire to have an English Bible that spoke to all the nation, transcending the religious divisions that had placed three different translations in the hands of his subjects. Internationally, he styled himself *Rex Pacificus* (the peace-loving king). In 1604, the Treaty of London brought Elizabeth's war with Spain formally to an end, and over the next decade he worked to bring about political marriages that might cement stable alliances. In 1613, he married his daughter to the leader of the German Protestants, while the following year he began discussions with Catholic Spain to marry his son to the Infanta Maria. After some ten years of negotiations, James's hopes for what was known as the Spanish match were finally abandoned, much to the delight of the nation, whose long-felt fear and hatred for Spain outweighed the subtle political logic behind the plan.

But if James sought stability and peace, and for the most part succeeded in his aims (at least until 1618, when the bitter religio-political conflicts on the European continent swirled well out of the King's control), he never really achieved concord and cohesion. He ruled over two kingdoms that did not know, like, or even want to understand one another, and his rule did little to bring them closer together. His England remained separate from his Scotland, even as he ruled over both. And even his England remained self divided, as in truth it always was under Elizabeth, ever more a nation of prosperity and influence but still one forged out of deep-rooted divisions of means, faiths, and allegiances that made the very nature of English identity a matter of confusion and concern. Arguably this is the very condition of great drama—sufficient peace and prosperity to support a theater industry and sufficient provocation in the troubling uncertainties about what the nation was and what fundamentally mattered to its people to inspire plays that would offer tentative solutions or at the very least make the troubling questions articulate and moving.

Nine years before James would die in 1625, Shakespeare died, having returned from London to the small market town in which he was born. If London, now a thriving modern metropolis of well over 200,000 people, had, like the nation itself, been transformed in the course of his life, the Warwickshire market town still was much the same. The house in which Shakespeare was born still stood, as did the church in which he was baptized and the school in which he learned to read and write. The river Avon still ran slowly along the town's southern limits. What had changed was that Shakespeare was now its most famous citizen, and, although it would take more than another 100 years to fully achieve this, he would in time become England's, for having turned the great ethical, social, and political issues of his own age into plays that would live forever.

William Shakespeare: A Chronology

1558	**November 17: Queen Elizabeth crowned**
1564	April 26: Shakespeare baptized, third child born to John Shakespeare and Mary Arden
1564	**May 27: Death of Jean Calvin in Geneva**
1565	John Shakespeare elected alderman in Stratford-upon-Avon
1568	**Publication of the Bishops' Bible**
1568	September 4: John Shakespeare elected Bailiff of Stratford-upon-Avon
1569	**Northern Rebellion**
1570	**Queen Elizabeth excommunicated by the Pope**
1572	**August 24: St. Bartholomew's Day Massacre in Paris**
1576	**The Theatre is built in Shoreditch**
1577–1580	**Sir Francis Drake sails around the world**
1582	November 27: Shakespeare and Anne Hathaway married (Shakespeare is 18)
1583	Queen's Men formed
1583	May 26: Shakespeare's daughter, Susanna, baptized
1584	**Failure of the Virginia Colony**

1585   February 2: Twins, Hamnet and Judith, baptized (Shakespeare is 20)

1586   Babington Plot to dethrone Elizabeth and replace her with Mary, Queen of Scots

1587   February 8: Execution of Mary, Queen of Scots

1587   Rose Theatre built

1588   August: Defeat of the Spanish armada (Shakespeare is 24)

1588   September 4: Death of Robert Dudley, Earl of Leicester

1590   First three books of Spenser's *Faerie Queene* published; Marlowe's *Tamburlaine* published

1592   March 3: *Henry VI, Part One* performed at the Rose Theatre (Shakespeare is 27)

1593   February–November: Theaters closed because of plague

1593   Publication of *Venus and Adonis*

1594   Publication of *Titus Andronicus*, first play by Shakespeare to appear in print (though anonymously)

1594   Lord Chamberlain's Men formed

1595   March 15: Payment made to Shakespeare, Will Kemp, and Richard Burbage for performances at court in December, 1594

1595   Swan Theatre built

1596   Books 4–6 of *The Faerie Queene* published

1596   August 11: Burial of Shakespeare's son, Hamnet (Shakespeare is 32)

1596–1599   Shakespeare living in St. Helen's, Bishopsgate, London

1596   October 20: Grant of Arms to John Shakespeare

1597   May 4: Shakespeare purchases New Place, one of the two largest houses in Stratford (Shakespeare is 33)

1598   Publication of *Love's Labor's Lost*, first extant play with Shakespeare's name on the title page

1598   Publication of Francis Meres's *Palladis Tamia*, citing Shakespeare as "the best for Comedy and Tragedy" among English writers

1599   Opening of the Globe Theatre

1601   February 7: Lord Chamberlain's Men paid 40 shillings to play *Richard II* by supporters of the Earl of Essex, the day before his abortive rebellion

1601   February 17: Execution of Robert Devereaux, Earl of Essex

1601   September 8: Burial of John Shakespeare

1602   May 1: Shakespeare buys 107 acres of farmland in Stratford

1603   March 24: Queen Elizabeth dies; James VI of Scotland succeeds as James I of England (Shakespeare is 39)

1603   May 19: Lord Chamberlain's Men reformed as the King's Men

1604   Shakespeare living with the Mountjoys, a French Huguenot family, in Cripplegate, London

1604   First edition of Marlowe's *Dr. Faustus* published (written c. 1589)

1604   March 15: Shakespeare named among "players" given scarlet cloth to wear at royal procession of King James

1604   Publication of authorized version of *Hamlet* (Shakespeare is 40)

1605   Gunpowder Plot

1605   June 5: Marriage of Susanna Shakespeare to John Hall

1608   Publication of *King Lear* (Shakespeare is 44)

1608–1609   Acquisition of indoor Blackfriars Theatre by King's Men

1609   *Sonnets* published

1611   King James Bible published (Shakespeare is 47)

1612   November 6: Death of Henry, eldest son of King James

1613   February 14: Marriage of King James's daughter Elizabeth to Frederick, the Elector Palatine

1613   March 10: Shakespeare, with some associates, buys gatehouse in Blackfriars, London

1613   June 29: Fire burns the Globe Theatre

1614   Rebuilt Globe reopens

1616   February 10: Marriage of Judith Shakespeare to Thomas Quiney

1616   March 25: Shakespeare's will signed

1616   April 23: Shakespeare dies (age 52)

1616   April 23: Cervantes dies in Madrid

1616   April 25: Shakespeare buried in Holy Trinity Church in Stratford-upon-Avon

1623   August 6: Death of Anne Shakespeare

1623   October: Prince Charles, King James's son, returns from Madrid, having failed to arrange his marriage to Maria Anna, Infanta of Spain

1623   First Folio published with 36 plays (18 never previously published)

Words, Words, Words: Understanding Shakespeare's Language
by David Scott Kastan

t is silly to pretend that it is easy to read Shakespeare. Reading Shakespeare isn't like picking up a copy of *USA Today* or *The New Yorker*, or even F. Scott Fitzgerald's *Great Gatsby* or Toni Morrison's *Beloved*. It is hard work, because the language is often unfamiliar to us and because it is more concentrated than we are used to. In the theater it is usually a bit easier. Actors can clarify meanings with gestures and actions, allowing us to get the general sense of what is going on, if not every nuance of the language that is spoken. "Action is eloquence," as Volumnia puts it in *Coriolanus*, "and the eyes of th' ignorant / More learnèd than the ears" (3.276–277). Yet the real greatness of Shakespeare rests not on "the general sense" of his plays but on the specificity and suggestiveness of the words in which they are written. It is through language that the plays' full dramatic power is realized, and it is that rich and robust language, often pushed by Shakespeare to the very limits of intelligibility, that we must learn to understand. But we can come to understand it (and enjoy it), and this essay is designed to help.

Even experienced readers and playgoers need help. They often find that his words are difficult to comprehend. Shakespeare sometimes uses words no longer current in English or with meanings that have changed. He regularly multiplies words where seemingly one might do as well or even better. He characteristically writes sentences that are syntactically complicated and imaginatively dense. And it isn't just we, removed by some 400 years from his world, who find him difficult to read; in his own time, his friends and fellow actors knew Shakespeare was hard. As two of them, John Hemings and Henry Condell, put it in their prefatory remarks to Shakespeare's First Folio in 1623, "read him, therefore, and again and again; and if then you do not like him, surely you are in some manifest danger not to understand him."

From the very beginning, then, it was obvious that the plays both deserve and demand not only careful reading but continued re-reading—and that not to read Shakespeare with all the attention a reader can bring to bear on the language is almost to guarantee that a reader will not "understand him" and remain among those who "do not like him." But Shakespeare's colleagues were nonetheless confident that the plays exerted an attraction strong enough to ensure and reward the concentration of their readers, confident, as they say, that in them "you will find enough, both to draw and hold you." The plays do exert a kind of magnetic pull, and have successfully drawn in and held readers for over 400 years.

Once we are drawn in, we confront a world of words that does not always immediately yield its delights; but it will—once we learn to see what is demanded of us. Words in Shakespeare do a lot, arguably more than anyone else has ever asked them to do. In part, it is because he needed his words to do many things at once. His stage had no sets and few props, so his words are all we have to enable us to imagine what his characters see. And they also allow us to see what the characters don't see, especially about themselves. The words are vivid and immediate, as well as complexly layered and psychologically suggestive. The difficulties they pose are not the "thee's" and "thou's" or "prithee's" and "doth's" that obviously mark the chronological distance between Shakespeare and us. When Gertrude says to Hamlet, "thou hast thy father much offended"

(3.4.8), we have no difficulty understanding her chiding, though we might miss that her use of the "thou" form of the pronoun expresses an intimacy that Hamlet pointedly refuses with his reply: "Mother, *you* have my father much offended" (3.4.9; italics mine).

Most deceptive are words that look the same as words we know but now mean something different. Words often change meanings over time. When Horatio and the soldiers try to stop Hamlet as he chases after the Ghost, Hamlet pushes past them and says, "I'll make a ghost of him that lets me" (1.4.85). It seems an odd thing to say. Why should he threaten someone who "lets" him do what he wants to do? But here "let" means "hinder," not, as it does today, "allow" (although the older meaning of the word still survives, for example, in tennis, where a "let serve" is one that is hindered by the net on its way across). There are many words that can, like this, mislead us: "his" sometimes means "its," "an" often means "if," "envy" means something more like "malice," "cousin" means more generally "kinsman," and there are others, though all are easily defined. The difficulty is that we may not stop to look thinking we already know what the word means, but in this edition a ° following the word alerts a reader that there is a gloss in the left margin, and quickly readers get used to these older meanings.

Then, of course, there is the intimidation factor—strange, polysyllabic, or Latinate words that not only are foreign to us but also must have sounded strange even to Shakespeare's audiences. When Macbeth wonders whether all the water in all the oceans of the world will be able to clean his bloody hands after the murder of Duncan, he concludes: "No; this my hand will rather / The multitudinous seas incarnadine, / Making the green one red" (2.2.64–66). Duncan's blood staining Macbeth's murderous hand is so offensive that, not merely does it resist being washed off in water, but it will "the multitudinous seas incarnadine": that is, turn the sea-green oceans blood-red. Notes will easily clarify the meaning of the two odd words, but it is worth observing that they would have been as odd to Shakespeare's readers as they are to us. The *Oxford English Dictionary* (*OED*) shows no use of "multitudinous" before this, and it records no use of "incarnadine" before 1591 (*Macbeth* was written about 1606). Both are new words, coined from the Latin, part of a process in Shakespeare's time where English adopted many Latinate words as a mark of its own emergence as an important vernacular language. Here they are used to express the magnitude of Macbeth's offense, a crime not only against the civil law but also against the cosmic order, and then the simple monosyllables of turning "the green one red" provide an immediate (and needed) paraphrase and register his own sickening awareness of the true hideousness of his deed.

As with "multitudinous" in *Macbeth*, Shakespeare is the source of a great many words in English. Sometimes he coined them himself, or, if he didn't invent them, he was the first person whose writing of them has survived. Some of these words have become part of our language, so common that it is hard to imagine they were not always part of it: for example, "assassination" (*Macbeth*, 1.7.2), "bed room" (*A Midsummer Night's Dream*, 2.2.57), "countless" (*Titus Andronicus*, 5.3.59), "fashionable" (*Troilus and Cressida*, 3.3.165), "frugal" (*The Merry Wives of Windsor*, 2.1.28), "laughable" (*The Merchant of Venice*, 1.1.56), "lonely" (*Coriolanus*, 4.1.30), and "useful" (*King John*, 5.2.81). But other words that he originated were not as, to use yet another Shakespearean coinage, "successful" (*Titus Andronicus*, 1.1.66). Words like "crimeless" (*Henry VI, Part Two*, 2.4.63, meaning "innocent"), "facinorous" (*All's Well That Ends Well*, 2.3.30, meaning "extremely wicked"), and "recountment" (*As You Like It*, 4.3.141, meaning "narrative" or "account") have, without much resistance, slipped into oblivion. Clearly Shakespeare liked words, even unwieldy ones. His working vocabulary, about 18,000 words, is staggering, larger than almost any other English writer, and he seems to be the first person to use in print about 1,000 of these. Whether he coined the new words himself or was intrigued by the new words he heard in the streets of London doesn't really matter; the point is that he was remarkably alert to and engaged with a dynamic language that was expanding in response to England's own expanding contact with the world around it.

But it is neither new words nor old ones that are the source of the greatest difficulty of Shakespeare's language. The real difficulty (and the real delight) comes in trying to see how he uses the words, how he endows them with more than their denotative meanings. Why, for example, does Macbeth say that he hopes that the "sure and firm-set earth" (2.1.56) will not hear his steps as he goes forward to murder Duncan? Here "sure" and "firm-set" mean virtually the same thing: stable, secure, fixed. Why use two words? If this were a student paper, no doubt the teacher would circle one of them and write "redundant." But the redundancy is exactly what Shakespeare wants. One word would do if the purpose were to describe the solidity of the earth, but here the redundancy points to something different. It reveals something about Macbeth's mind, betraying through the doubling how deep is his awareness of the world of stable values that the terrible act he is about to commit must unsettle.

Shakespeare's words usually work this way: in part describing what the characters see and as often betraying what they feel. The example from *Macbeth* is a simple example of how this works. Shakespeare's words are carefully patterned. How one says something is every bit as important as what is said, and the conspicuous patterns that are created alert us to the fact that something more than the words' lexical sense has been put into play. Words can be coupled, as in the example above, or knit into even denser metaphorical constellations to reveal something about the speaker (which often the speaker does not know), as in Prince Hal's promise to his father that he will outdo the rebels' hero, Henry Percy (Hotspur):

Percy is but my factor, good my lord,

To engross up glorious deeds on my behalf.

And I will call him to so strict account

That he shall render every glory up,

Yea, even the slightest worship of his time,

Or I will tear the reckoning from his heart.

(Henry IV, Part One, 3.2.147–152)

The Prince expresses his confidence that he will defeat Hotspur, but revealingly in a reiterated language of commercial exchange ("factor," "engross," "account," "render," "reckoning") that tells us something important both about the Prince and the ways in which he understands his world. In a play filled with references to coins and counterfeiting, the speech demonstrates not only that Hal has committed himself to the business at hand, repudiating his earlier, irresponsible tavern self, but also that he knows it is a business rather than a glorious world of chivalric achievement; he inhabits a world in which value (political as well as economic) is not intrinsic but determined by what people are willing to invest, and he proves himself a master of producing desire for what he has to offer.

Or sometimes it is not the network of imagery but the very syntax that speaks, as when Claudius announces his marriage to Hamlet's mother:

Therefore our sometime sister, now our Queen,

Th' imperial jointress to this warlike state,

Have we—as 'twere with a defeated joy,

With an auspicious and a dropping eye,

With mirth in funeral and with dole in marriage,

In equal scale weighing delight and dole—

Taken to wife.   *(Hamlet, 1.2.8–14)*

All he really wants to say here is that he has married Gertrude, his former sister-in-law: "Therefore our sometime sister . . . Have we . . . Taken to wife." But the straightforward sentence gets interrupted and complicated, revealing his own discomfort with the announcement. His elaborations and intensifications of Gertrude's role ("sometime sister," "Queen," "imperial jointress"), the self-conscious rhetorical balancing of the middle three lines (indeed "in equal scale weighing delight and dole"), all declare by the all-too obvious artifice how desperate he is to hide the awkward facts behind a veneer of normalcy and propriety. The very unnaturalness of the sentence is what alerts us that we are meant to understand more than the simple relation of fact.

Why doesn't Shakespeare just say what he means? Well, he does—exactly what he means. In the example from *Hamlet* just above, Shakespeare shows us something about Claudius that Claudius doesn't know himself. Always Shakespeare's words will offer us an immediate sense of what is happening, allowing us to follow the action, but they also offer us a counterplot, pointing us to what might be behind the action, confirming or contradicting what the characters say. It is a language that shimmers with promise and possibility, opening the characters' hearts and minds to our view—and all we have to do is learn to pay attention to what is there before us.

Shakespeare's Verse

Another distinctive feature of Shakespeare's dramatic language is that much of it is in verse. Almost all of the plays mix poetry and prose, but the poetry dominates. *The Merry Wives of Windsor* has the lowest percentage (only about 13 percent verse), while *Richard II* and *King John* are written entirely in verse (the only examples, although *Henry VI, Part One* and *Part Three* have only a very few prose lines). In most of the plays, about 70 percent of the lines are written in verse.

Shakespeare's characteristic verse line is a non-rhyming iambic pentameter ("blank verse"), ten syllables with every second one stressed. In *A Midsummer Night's Dream*, Titania comes to her senses after a magic potion has led her to fall in love with an ass-headed Bottom: "Methought I was enamored of an ass" (4.1.76). Similarly, in *Romeo and Juliet*, Romeo gazes up at Juliet's window: "But soft, what light through yonder window breaks" (2.2.2). In both these examples, the line has ten syllables organized into five regular beats (each beat consisting of the stress on the second syllable of a pair, as in "But soft," the da-dum rhythm forming an "iamb"). Still, we don't hear these lines as jingles; they seem natural enough, in large part because this dominant pattern is varied in the surrounding lines.

The play of stresses indeed becomes another key to meaning, as Shakespeare alerts us to what is important. In *Measure for Measure*, Lucio urges Isabella to plead for her brother's life: "Oh, to him, to him, wench! He will relent" (2.2.129). The iambic norm (unstressed-stressed) tells us (and an actor) that the emphasis at the beginning of the line is on "to" not "him"—it is the action not the object that is being emphasized—and at the end of the line the stress falls on "will." Alternatively, the line can play against the established norm. In *Hamlet*, Claudius corrects Polonius's idea of what is bothering the Prince: "Love? His affections do not that way tend" (3.1.161). The iambic norm forces the emphasis onto "that" ("do not *that* way tend"), while the syntax forces an unexpected stress on the opening word, "Love." In the famous line, "The course of true love never did run smooth" (*A Midsummer Night's Dream*, 1.1.134), the iambic expectation is varied in both the middle and at the end of the line. Both "love" and the first syllable of "never" are stressed, as are both syllables at the end—"run smooth"—which creates a metrical foot in which both syllables are stressed (called a "spondee"). The point to notice is that the "da-dum, da-dum, da-dum, da-dum, da-dum" line is not inevitable; it merely sets an expectation against which many variations can be heard.

In fact, even the ten-syllable norm can be varied. Shakespeare sometimes writes lines with fewer or more syllables. Often there is an extra, unstressed syllable at the end of a line (a so-called "feminine ending"); sometimes there are verse lines with only nine. In *Henry IV, Part One*, King Henry replies incredulously to the rebel Worcester's claim that he hadn't "sought" the confrontation with the King: "You have not sought it. How comes it then?" (5.1.27). There are only nine syllables here (some earlier editors, seeking to "correct" the verse, added the word "sir" after the first question to regularize the line). But the pause where one expects a stressed syllable is dramatically effective, allowing the King's anger to be powerfully present in the silence.

As even these few examples show, Shakespeare's verse is unusually flexible, allowing a range of rhythmical effects. It should not be understood as a set of strict rules but as a flexible set of practices rooted in dramatic necessity. It is designed to highlight ideas and emotions, and it is based less upon rigid syllable counts than on an arrangement of stresses within an understood temporal norm, as one might expect from a poetry written to be heard in the theater rather than read on the page.

Here Follows Prose

Although the plays are dominated by verse, prose plays a significant role. Shakespeare's prose has its own rhythms, but it lacks the formal patterning of verse, and so is printed without line breaks and without the capitals that mark the beginning of a verse line. Like many of his fellow dramatists, Shakespeare tended to use prose for comic scenes, the shift from verse serving, especially in his early plays, as a social marker. Upper-class characters speak in verse; lower-class characters speak in prose. Thus, in *A Midsummer Night's Dream*, the Athenians of the court, as well as the fairies, all speak in verse, but the "rude mechanicals," Bottom and his artisan friends, all speak in prose, except for the comic verse they speak in their performance of "Pyramis and Thisbe."

As Shakespeare grew in experience, he became more flexible about the shifts from verse to prose, letting it, among other things, mark genre rather than class and measure various kinds of intensity. Prose becomes in the main the medium of comedy. The great comedies, like *Much Ado About Nothing*, *Twelfth Night*, and *As You Like It*, are all more than 50 percent prose. But even in comedy, shifts between verse and prose may be used to measure subtle emotional changes. In Act One, scene three of *The Merchant of Venice*, Shylock and Bassanio begin the scene speaking of matters of business in prose, but when Antonio enters and the deep conflict between the Christian and the Jew becomes evident, the scene shifts to verse. But prose may itself serve in moments of emotional intensity. Shylock's famous speech in Act Three, scene one, "Hath not a Jew eyes . . ." is all in prose, as is Hamlet's expression of disgust at the world ("I have of late—but wherefore I know not—lost all my mirth . . .") at 3.1.51–64. Shakespeare comes to use prose to vary the tone of a scene, as the shift from verse subtly alerts an audience or a reader to some new emotional register.

Prose becomes, as Shakespeare's art matures, not inevitably the mark of the lower classes but the mark of a salutary daily-ness. It is appropriately the medium in which letters are written, and it is the medium of a common sense that will at least challenge the potential self-deceptions of grandiloquent speech. When Rosalind mocks the excesses and artifice of Orlando's wooing in Act Four, scene one of *As You Like It*, it is in prose that she seeks something genuine in the expression of love:

The poor world is almost six thousand years old, and in all this time there was not any man died in his own person, *videlicit* [i.e., namely], in a love cause. . . . Men have died from time to time, and worms have eaten them, but not for love.

Here the prose becomes the sound of common sense, an effective foil to the affectation of pinning poems to trees and thinking that it is real love.

It is not that prose is artless; Shakespeare's prose is no less self-conscious than his verse. The artfulness of his prose is different, of course. The seeming ordinariness of his prose is no less an effect of his artistry than is the more obvious patterning of his verse. Prose is no less serious, compressed, or indeed figurative. As with his verse, Shakespeare's prose performs numerous tasks and displays various, subtle formal qualities; and recognizing the possibilities of what it can achieve is still another way of seeing what Shakespeare puts right before us to show us what he has hidden.

Further Reading

N. F. Blake, *Shakespeare's Language: An Introduction* (New York: St. Martin's Press, 1983).

Jonathan Hope, *Shakespeare's Grammar* (London: Thomson, 2003).

Sister Miriam Joseph, *Shakespeare's Use of the Arts of Language* (New York: Columbia University Press, 1947).

M. M. Mahood, *Shakespeare's Wordplay* (London: Methuen, 1957).

Russ McDonald, *Shakespeare and the Arts of Language* (Oxford: Oxford University Press, 2001).

Brian Vickers, *The Artistry of Shakespeare's Prose* (London: Methuen, 1968).

George T. Wright, *Shakespeare's Metrical Art* (Berkeley: Univ. of California Press, 1991).

Key to the Play Text

Symbols

°   Indicates an explanation or definition in the
left-hand margin.

¹   Indicates a gloss on the page facing the play text.

[ ]   Indicates something added or changed by the editors
(i.e., not in the early printed text that this edition
of the play is based on).

Terms

Q1, Q2, or   *Quarto* refers to a small inexpensive format in which
Quarto   individual play books were usually published. *The
Merchant of Venice* was published in quarto in 1600 and
again in 1619, and this edition is based on the 1600
publication.

F, Folio, or   The first collected edition of Shakespeare's plays,
First Folio   published in 1623.

The Merchant of Venice

William Shakespeare

List of Roles

Antonio		*a wealthy Venetian merchant*
Bassanio		*his friend and suitor to Portia*
Gratiano	⎫	
Solanio	⎪	*Venetian gentlemen and friends*
Salarino	⎬	*of Antonio and Bassanio*
Salerio	⎪	
Lorenzo	⎭	
Leonardo		*Bassanio's servant*

Portia		*a wealthy heiress in Belmont*
Nerissa		*her waiting gentlewoman*
Balthazar	⎫	*Portia's servants*
Stephano	⎭	
Morocco	⎫	*princes and suitors to Portia*
Aragon	⎭	

Shylock	*a rich Jewish moneylender*
Jessica	*his daughter, in love with Lorenzo*
Launcelot Gobbo	*his servant and later Bassanio's*
Gobbo	*Launcelot's father*
Tubal	*a Jewish moneylender*

Duke of Venice
Servingman
Messenger
Man
Singer

Magnificoes, court officers, followers, servants, and attendants

1   *such a want-wit sadness makes of me /*
    That I have much ado to know myself

    **Sadness makes me such a fool that
    it is difficult for me to understand
    my own emotions.**

2   *portly*

    **Stately, fat bellied (because they are
    filled with wind)**

3   *signiors and rich burghers*

    Gentlemen and rich citizens

4   *Do overpeer the petty traffickers / That
    curtsy to them, do them reverence / As
    they fly by them with their woven wings*

    **Look down upon the smaller mer-
    chant ships that, bobbing up and
    down on the water, seem to bow to
    Antonio's ships as they sail by**

5   *The better part of my affections would /
    Be with my hopes abroad*

    **The majority of my thoughts would
    be with my business ventures
    abroad.**

6   *Plucking the grass to know where sits the
    wind*

    **Pulling up and tossing pieces of
    grass to see from which direction
    the wind was blowing**

7   *piers and roads*

    Harbors and sheltered coves

8   *out of doubt*

    Certainly

9   *My wind cooling my broth / Would blow
    me to an ague when I thought / What
    harm a wind too great might do at sea.*

    **Blowing on my soup to cool it
    down would make me shiver, as it
    reminded me of how much damage
    a big wind at sea could do (to my
    ships).**

10 *sandy hourglass run*

    **I.e., sands pass through my hour-
    glass**

Act 1, Scene 1

Enter **Antonio**, **Salarino**, *and* **Solanio**.

Antonio

_{truth} In sooth° I know not why I am so sad.

It wearies me; you say it wearies you.

But how I caught it, found it, or came by it,

What stuff 'tis made of, whereof it is born,

_{have yet} I am° to learn,   5

And such a want-wit sadness makes of me

That I have much ado to know myself. [1]

Salarino

Your mind is tossing on the ocean,

_{merchant ships} There where your argosies° with portly[2] sail

_{sea} (Like signiors and rich burghers[3] on the flood°   10

Or, as it were, the pageants of the sea)

_{insignificant} Do overpeer the petty° traffickers

That curtsy to them, do them reverence

As they fly by them with their woven wings. [4]

Solanio

_{a risky investment} Believe me, sir, had I such venture° forth,   15

The better part of my affections would

_{always} Be with my hopes abroad.[5] I should be still°

Plucking the grass to know where sits the wind,[6]

Peering in maps for ports and piers and roads, [7]

And every object that might make me fear   20

Misfortune to my ventures out of doubt[8]

Would make me sad.

Salarino

_{breath}   My wind° cooling my broth

_{fever} Would blow me to an ague° when I thought

What harm a wind too great might do at sea. [9]

I should not see the sandy hourglass run [10]   25

43

1 Andrew

The name of Salarino's ship

2 *docked in sand, / Vailing her high top*
   lower than her ribs / To kiss her burial

**Salarino imagines that his ship has
run aground and the tallest mast
has fallen over into the sand.**

3 *spices*

**I.e., the cargo that the ship was
carrying**

4 *but even now worth this / And now worth*
   nothing

**The cargo that was recently so
valuable (*this* may be accompanied
by a gesture to indicate the value)
is now worth nothing, since it has
been ruined in the shipwreck.**

5 *Shall I have the thought / To think on this,*
   and shall I lack the thought / That such a
   thing bechanced would make me sad?

**I.e., can I think about this possibil-
ity without thinking about how
disastrous such an event would be
for me?**

6 *nor is my whole estate / Upon the fortune*
   of this present year

**Nor have I risked the entirety of my
wealth on the outcome of this current undertaking**

7 *two-headed Janus*

**Roman god who had two faces,
one looking forward and the other
looking backward, and here pointing at the possibility of either good
or bad fortune**

8 *peep through their eyes*

Squint their eyes in laughter

9 *laugh like parrots at a bagpiper*

**I.e., laugh loudly and foolishly at
something that is not funny**

sandbars	But I should think of shallows and of flats,°
	And see my wealthy *Andrew*[1] docked in sand,
	Vailing her high top lower than her ribs
	To kiss her burial.[2] Should I go to church
	And see the holy edifice of stone 30
immediately	And not bethink me straight° of dangerous rocks,
merely	Which, touching but° my gentle vessel's side,
sea	Would scatter all her spices[3] on the stream,°
	Enrobe the roaring waters with my silks,
	And, in a word, but even now worth this 35
	And now worth nothing?[4] Shall I have the thought
	To think on this, and shall I lack the thought
	That such a thing bechanced would make me sad?[5]
	But tell not me; I know Antonio
business	Is sad to think upon his merchandise.° 40

Antonio

	Believe me, no. I thank my fortune for it,
ship's hull	My ventures are not in one bottom° trusted,
destination	Nor to one place,° nor is my whole estate
	Upon the fortune of this present year.[6]
	Therefore my merchandise makes me not sad. 45

Solanio

Why, then you are in love.

Antonio

<table><tr><td>*No; For shame*</td><td>Fie,° fie!</td></tr></table>

Solanio

	Not in love neither? Then let us say you are sad
	Because you are not merry—and 'twere as easy
	For you to laugh and leap and say you are merry
	Because you are not sad. Now, by two-headed Janus,[7] 50
created	Nature hath framed° strange fellows in her time:
always	Some that will evermore° peep through their eyes[8]
	And laugh like parrots at a bagpiper,[9]

1   *vinegar aspect*

Sour expression

2   *Nestor*

A Greek leader during the Trojan War noted for his experience and wisdom

3   *when shall we laugh?*

I.e., when will we have some fun together?

4   *exceeding strange*

Very distant

5   *We'll make our leisures to attend on yours.*

I.e., we're ready when you are.

6   *have in mind*

Remember

others   And other° of such vinegar aspect¹

That they'll not show their teeth in way of smile   55

Even if   Though° Nestor² swear the jest be laughable.

Enter **Bassanio**, **Lorenzo**, *and* **Gratiano**.

Here comes Bassanio, your most noble kinsman,

Gratiano, and Lorenzo. Fare ye well.

We leave you now with better company.

Salarino

I would have stayed till I had made you merry   60

If worthier friends had not prevented me.

Antonio

Your worth is very dear in my regard.

I take it your own business calls on you,

welcome   And you embrace° th' occasion to depart.

Salarino

morning   [*to* **Bassanio**, **Lorenzo**, **Gratiano**] Good morrow,° my

    good lords.   65

Bassanio

[*to* **Salarino** *and* **Solanio**] Good signiors both, when

    shall we laugh?³ Say, when?

You grow exceeding strange.⁴ Must it be so?

Salarino

We'll make our leisures to attend on yours.⁵

            Salarino *and* **Solanio** *exit.*

Lorenzo

My Lord Bassanio, since you have found Antonio,

We two will leave you. But at dinnertime   70

I pray you have in mind⁶ where we must meet.

Bassanio

I will not fail you.

1   *respect upon*

    Concern for

2   *They lose it that do buy it with much care.*

    One who worries too much about how to achieve his fortune will be unable to enjoy the pleasures it can provide him.

3   *let my liver rather heat with wine / Than my heart cool with mortifying groans*

    Let me become excited by merry drinking, rather than penitent with groans of self-denial.

4   *his grandsire cut in alabaster*

    The memorial sculpture on his grandfather's grave (*alabaster* is a smooth white stone often used for carving)

5   *creep into the jaundice / By being peevish*

    Give himself jaundice (a disease of the liver) by being irritable

6   *Do cream and mantle like a standing pond*

    Have an expression fixed on their faces like algae coating a stagnant pond

7   *do a willful stillness entertain / With purpose to be dressed in an opinion / Of wisdom, gravity, profound conceit*

    Intentionally remain silent so that they might earn the reputation for wisdom, seriousness, and deep understanding; see Proverbs 17:28: "Even a fool, when he holdeth his peace, is counted wise."

8   *"I am Sir Oracle, / And when I ope my lips, let no dog bark!"*

    A joke; these men wish to be thought so wise that when they speak even dogs fall silent to listen.

9   *If they should speak would almost damn those ears / Which, hearing them, would call their brothers fools*

    I.e., If those men were to speak, their listeners would be in danger of damnation, for they would have to call the speakers fools. According to the Bible, "whosoever shall say unto his brother . . . thou fool, shall be in danger of Hell fire" (Matthew 5:22).

Gratiano

You look not well, Signior Antonio.

You have too much respect upon° the world.

They lose it that do buy it with much care.°   75

Believe me, you are marvelously changed.

Antonio

value/merely I hold° the world but° as the world, Gratiano:

A stage where every man must play a part,

And mine a sad one.

Gratiano

                                   Let me play the fool.

With mirth and laughter let old wrinkles come,   80

And let my liver rather heat with wine

Than my heart cool with mortifying groans.°

Why should a man whose blood is warm within

Sit like his grandsire cut in alabaster,°

should be awake Sleep when he wakes,° and creep into the jaundice   85

By being peevish?° I tell thee what, Antonio.

I love thee, and 'tis my love that speaks:

faces There are a sort of men whose visages°

Do cream and mantle like a standing pond°

And do a willful stillness entertain   90

With purpose to be dressed in an opinion

Of wisdom, gravity, profound conceit,°

As who should say, "I am Sir Oracle,

And when I ope my lips, let no dog bark!"°

O my Antonio, I do know of these   95

thought to be That therefore only are reputed° wise

For saying nothing, when, I am very sure,

If they should speak would almost damn those ears

Which, hearing them, would call their brothers fools.°

I'll tell thee more of this another time,   100

1   *But fish not with this melancholy bait /*
    For this fool gudgeon, this opinion

    I.e., do not pretend to be melancholy to trick gullible men into thinking that you are wise. (A *gudgeon* is a small fresh-water fish notorious for eating anything, hence a gullible person.)

2   *I'll grow a talker for this gear.*

    I'll become a talker, having heard this chatter (*gear*) of yours.

3   *maid not vendible*

    A woman who is not marriageable

4   *Is that anything now?*

    I.e., has Gratiano yet said anything worthwhile?

5   *chaff*

    Inedible husks of the wheat plant

But fish not with this melancholy bait
For this fool gudgeon, this opinion.[1]
—Come, good Lorenzo.—Fare ye well awhile.
I'll end my exhortation after dinner.

Lorenzo

Well, we will leave you then till dinnertime.   105
silent   I must be one of these same dumb° wise men,
For Gratiano never lets me speak.

Gratiano

i.e., if you keep   Well, keep° me company but two years more,
Thou shalt not know the sound of thine own tongue.

Antonio

Fare you well. I'll grow a talker for this gear.[2]   110

Gratiano

Thanks, i' faith, for silence is only commendable
ox's   In a neat's° tongue dried and a maid not vendible.[3]

                              [**Gratiano** *and* **Lorenzo**] *exit.*

Antonio

Is that anything now?[4]

Bassanio

Gratiano speaks an infinite deal of nothing, more than
sensible points   any man in all Venice. His reasons° are as two grains   115
of wheat hid in two bushels of chaff:[5] you shall seek all
before   day ere° you find them, and when you have them they
are not worth the search.

Antonio

Well, tell me now what lady is the same
To whom you swore a secret pilgrimage   120
That you today promised to tell me of?

Bassanio

'Tis not unknown to you, Antonio,
squandered   How much I have disabled° mine estate

1 *By something showing a more swelling*
   port / Than my faint means would grant
   continuance

   **By living a somewhat more lavish
   lifestyle than my meager funds
   would allow**

2 *make moan to be abridged / From such a*
   noble rate

   **Complain about having to give up
   my extravagant way of life**

3 *come fairly off from*

   Pay off honorably

4 *his fellow of the selfsame flight*

   An arrow of equal size and weight

5 *and by adventuring both, / I oft found*
   both.

   **By risking both, I often recovered
   both. (Bassanio proposes to pay off
   his debts to Antonio by first borrowing more money.)**

6 *pure innocence*

   I.e., not a trick

7 *latter hazard*

   I.e., second loan

By something showing a more swelling port

Than my faint means would grant continuance.[1]   125

Nor do I now make moan to be abridged

concern   From such a noble rate.[2] But my chief care°

Is to come fairly off from[3] the great debts

past / wasteful   Wherein my time,° something too prodigal,°

obligated to pay   Hath left me gaged.° To you, Antonio,   130

I owe the most in money and in love,

authorization   And from your love I have a warranty°

reveal   To unburden° all my plots and purposes

How to get clear of all the debts I owe.

Antonio

I pray you, good Bassanio, let me know it,   135

And, if it stand, as you yourself still do,

Within the eye of honor, be assured

My purse, my person, my extremest means

needs   Lie all unlocked to your occasions.°

Bassanio

arrow   In my school days, when I had lost one shaft,°   140

I shot his fellow of the selfsame flight[4]

careful   The selfsame way with more advisèd° watch

To find the other forth—and by adventuring both,

I oft found both.[5] I urge this childhood proof

Because what follows is pure innocence.[6]   145

I owe you much, and, like a willful youth,

That which I owe is lost; but if you please

same   To shoot another arrow that self° way

Which you did shoot the first, I do not doubt,

either   As I will watch the aim, or° to find both   150

Or bring your latter hazard[7] back again,

remain   And thankfully rest° debtor for the first.

1   *spend but time / To wind about my love with circumstance*

Only waste time by speaking about my love so circuitously (or "as if there were factors limiting it")

2   *making question of my uttermost*

Questioning my total commitment

3   *made waste of*

Squandered

4   *richly left*

With a large inherited fortune

5   *nothing undervalued*

Of no less worth than

6   *Cato's daughter, Brutus' Portia*

Portia, the daughter of the Roman statesman Cato, was married to Brutus, Julius Caesar's assassin. She became a familiar emblem of female excellence.

7   *like a golden fleece*

Portia's blonde hair is likened to the golden fleece of Greek legend, which Jason went in search of with his crewmen the Argonauts. Portia's home, Belmont, is thus equated with *Colchis* on the Black Sea (where Jason found the fleece), and her suitors are portrayed as *many Jasons* striving to win the treasure.

8   *hold a rival place*

Compete equally

9   *furnish thee*

Equip you to go

Antonio

You know me well, and herein spend but time
To wind about my love with circumstance, [1]
And out of doubt you do me now more wrong   155
In making question of my uttermost [2]
Than if you had made waste of [3] all I have.
merely Then do but° say to me what I should do
That in your knowledge may by me be done,
compelled And I am pressed° unto it. Therefore speak.   160

Bassanio

In Belmont is a lady richly left, [4]
And she is fair and—fairer than that word—
Once Of wondrous virtues. Sometimes° from her eyes
wordless I did receive fair speechless° messages.
Her name is Portia, nothing undervalued [5]   165
To Cato's daughter, Brutus' Portia. [6]
Nor is the wide world ignorant of her worth,
For the four winds blow in from every coast
Renownèd suitors, and her sunny locks
Hang on her temples like a golden fleece, [7]   170
residence/shore Which makes her seat° of Belmont Colchis' strand,°
And many Jasons come in quest of her.
O my Antonio, had I but the means
To hold a rival place [8] with one of them,
foretells/profit I have a mind presages° me such thrift°   175
assuredly That I should questionless° be fortunate.

Antonio

Thou know'st that all my fortunes are at sea.
goods Neither have I money nor commodity°
To raise a present sum. Therefore go forth;
Try what my credit can in Venice do—   180
stretched That shall be racked° even to the uttermost
To furnish thee [9] to Belmont, to fair Portia.

1   *I no question make / To have it of my trust*
    or for my sake

    I am sure that we can borrow the
    money, either upon my credit or
    from my friends.

immediately   Go presently° inquire, and so will I,
Where money is, and I no question make
To have it of my trust or for my sake.'   185

They exit.

1   *Superfluity comes sooner by white hairs,*
    but competency lives longer.

    Excess quickly ages a person, but
    moderation prolongs life.

2   *chapels had been churches*

    I.e., more people would be wor-
    shipping God (and small *chapels*
    would have to be replaced by larger
    ***churches*).**

3   *The brain may devise laws for the blood,*
    but a hot temper leaps o'er a cold decree.

    The brain may try to regulate hu-
    man emotions, but a passionate
    disposition will ignore the sober
    laws (set by reason).

4   *Such a hare is madness the youth to*
    skip o'er the meshes of good counsel the
    cripple.

    Portia compares youth to a wild
    hare: just as the hare manages to
    avoid the *meshes* (traps) set out
    for it, young people ignore the
    restraints that the *good counsel of the*
    ***cripple* (i.e., the good advice of the**
    elderly) set upon their behavior.

5   *in the fashion*

    Of a sort

6   *will*

    Both "desire" and "testament"

Act 1, Scene 2

Enter **Portia** *with her waiting woman* **Nerissa**.

Portia

faith By my troth,° Nerissa, my little body is aweary of this
great world.

Nerissa

You would be, sweet madam, if your miseries were in
the same abundance as your good fortunes are, and yet,
anything / overeat for aught° I see, they are as sick that surfeit° with too   5
small much as they that starve with nothing. It is no mean°
middle happiness, therefore, to be seated in the mean.°
Superfluity comes sooner by white hairs, but compe-
tency lives longer.[1]

Portia

sayings / spoken Good sentences,° and well pronounced.°   10

Nerissa

They would be better if well followed.

Portia

If to do were as easy as to know what were good to do,
chapels had been churches,[2] and poor men's cottages
clergyman princes' palaces. It is a good divine° that follows his
own instructions. I can easier teach twenty what were   15
good to be done than to be one of the twenty to follow
mine own teaching. The brain may devise laws for the
blood, but a hot temper leaps o'er a cold decree.[3] Such
a hare is madness the youth to skip o'er the meshes of
good counsel the cripple.[4] But this reasoning is not in   20
the fashion[5] to choose me a husband. O me, the word
want "choose!" I may neither choose who I would° nor refuse
desire who I dislike—so is the will° of a living daughter
curbed by the will[6] of a dead father. Is it not hard,
Nerissa, that I cannot choose one nor refuse none?   25

1   *overname them*

    Go through their names

2   *colt*

    **Silly young person, with a pun
    alluding to the prince's
    preoccupation with horses**

3   *played false with a smith*

    Had an affair with a blacksmith

4   *as who should say, "An you will not have
    me, choose"*

    **As if to say, "If you do not want me,
    do as you please."**

5   *prove the weeping philosopher*

    **Turn out like Heraclitus of Ephesus
    (500 B.C.), the melancholy
    philosopher who wept at the
    follies of others**

Nerissa

always Your father was ever° virtuous, and holy men at their
death have good inspirations. Therefore the lottery
that he hath devised in these three chests of gold,
i.e., Portia's father's silver, and lead, whereof who chooses his° meaning
chooses you, will no doubt never be chosen by any   30
rightly but one who you shall rightly love. But what
warmth is there in your affection towards any of these
princely suitors that are already come?

Portia

I pray thee, overname them,¹ and, as thou namest
them, I will describe them, and, according to my   35
guess description, level° at my affection.

Nerissa

First, there is the Neapolitan prince.

Portia

Ay, that's a colt² indeed, for he doth nothing but talk of
considers / addition his horse, and he makes° it a great appropriation° to
qualities his own good parts° that he can shoe him himself. I   40
am much afeard my lady his mother played false with
a smith.³

Nerissa

Count Then is there the County° Palatine.

Portia

If He doth nothing but frown, as who should say, "An°
you will not have me, choose."⁴ He hears merry tales   45
and smiles not. I fear he will prove the weeping philoso-
inappropriate pher⁵ when he grows old, being so full of unmannerly°
sadness in his youth. I had rather be married to a
skull death's-head° with a bone in his mouth than to either
of these. God defend me from these two!   50

Nerissa

concerning How say you by° the French lord, Monsieur le Bon?

1 *He is every man in no man.*

   I.e., by imitating everyone else, Monsieur le Bon has no character of his own.

2 *falls straight a-cap'ring*

   Immediately begins dancing

3 *He is a proper man's picture*

   I.e., he looks handsome.

4 *dumb show*

   Pantomime

5 *round hose*

   Puffy trousers

6 *he borrowed a box of the ear of the Englishman*

   He was punched on the side of the head by the Englishman.

7 *the Frenchman became his surety and sealed under for another*

   I.e., the French lord promised to back him up and promised also to punch the Englishman on his own. The joke here concerns the periodic alliances of the Scots and the French against the English.

Portia

God made him, and therefore let him pass for a man.
In truth, I know it is a sin to be a mocker, but he! Why,
he hath a horse better than the Neapolitan's, a better
bad habit of frowning than the Count Palatine. He is   55
thrush every man in no man.[1] If a throstle° sing, he falls
straight a-cap'ring.[2] He will fence with his own
shadow. If I should marry him, I should marry twenty
husbands. If he would despise me I would forgive him,
repay (i.e., love) for if he love me to madness I shall never requite° him.   60

Nerissa

What say you then to Falconbridge, the young baron
of England?

Portia

You know I say nothing to him, for he understands not
me, nor I him. He hath neither Latin, French, nor Ital-
court of law ian, and you will come into the court° and swear that I   65
have a poor pennyworth in the English. He is a proper
man's picture,[3] but, alas, who can converse with a
dressed dumb show?[4] How oddly he is suited!° I think he bought
jacket his doublet° in Italy, his round hose[5] in France, his
hat bonnet° in Germany, and his behavior everywhere.   70

Nerissa

What think you of the Scottish lord, his neighbor?

Portia

That he hath a neighborly charity in him, for he borrowed a box of the ear of the Englishman[6] and swore
he would pay him again when he was able. I think the
Frenchman became his surety and sealed under for   75
another.[7]

Nerissa

How like you the young German, the Duke of Saxony's
nephew?

1 *An the worst fall that ever fell, I hope I*
   shall make shift to go without him.

   If the worst that could happen
   should befall, I hope I can manage
   to avoid marrying him.

2 *Rhenish wine*

   German white wine (see 3.1.35)

3 *Sibylla*

   The Cumean *Sybil* (prophetess) of
   classical myth, to whom Apollo
   granted as many years of life as the
   grains of sand she could hold in
   one hand

4 *Diana*

   The Roman goddess of chastity

Portia

Very vilely in the morning, when he is sober, and most
vilely in the afternoon, when he is drunk. When he   80
is best he is a little worse than a man, and when he is
If   worst he is little better than a beast. An° the worst fall
that ever fell, I hope I shall make shift to go without
him.[1]

Nerissa

If he should offer to choose and choose the right casket,   85
be refusing   you should refuse° to perform your father's will if you
should refuse to accept him.

Portia

Therefore, for fear of the worst, I pray thee, set a deep
wrong   glass of Rhenish wine[2] on the contrary° casket, for
if the devil be within and that temptation without, I   90
know he will choose it. I will do anything, Nerissa, ere
i.e., drunkard   I will be married to a sponge.°

Nerissa

You need not fear, lady, the having any of these lords.
intentions   They have acquainted me with their determinations,°
which is indeed to return to their home and to trouble   95
you with no more suit unless you may be won by some
means   other sort° than your father's imposition depending
on the caskets.

Portia

If I live to be as old as Sibylla,[3] I will die as chaste as
Diana[4] unless I be obtained by the manner of my father's   100
group   will. I am glad this parcel° of wooers are so reason-
able, for there is not one among them but I dote on
his very absence, and I pray God grant them a fair
departure.

1   *Montferrat*

A well-known Italian noble family name (Monferrato) that Shakespeare might have known about from Boccaccio's *Decameron*

2   *shrive me*

Hear my confession and absolve my sins

3   *Sirrah*

Term of address usually used for a person of inferior social rank

Nerissa

Do you not remember, lady, in your father's time a   105
Venetian, a scholar and a soldier, that came hither in
company of the Marquess of Montferrat?[1]

Portia

Yes, yes, it was Bassanio—as I think so was he called.

Nerissa

True, madam. He, of all the men that ever my foolish
eyes looked upon, was the best deserving a fair lady.   110

Portia

I remember him well, and I remember him worthy of
thy praise.

Enter a **Servingman**.

How now, what news?

Servingman

The four strangers seek for you, madam, to take their
messenger leave; and there is a forerunner° come from a fifth, the   115
Prince of Morocco, who brings word the Prince his
master will be here tonight.

Portia

If I could bid the fifth welcome with so good heart as
I can bid the other four farewell, I should be glad of his
character approach. If he have the condition° of a saint and the   120
complexion of a devil, I had rather he should shrive
marry me[2] than wive° me.
Come, Nerissa. [*to the* **Servingman**] Sirrah,[3] go before.
Whiles we shut the gate upon one wooer,
Another knocks at the door.   *They exit.*   125

1   *well*

As in line 5, Shylock uses *well* to mean "I understand," as he considers the terms of the proposal.

2   *bound*

Obligated by contract to pay

3   *sufficient*

Sufficiently wealthy (to act as your guarantor)

4   *in supposition*

Questionable

5   *Tripoli*

A major port in modern Lebanon

6   *the Rialto*

The central bridge in Venice, the *Ponte di Rialto*, on one end of which was the Exchange, where most financial transactions were conducted

Act 1, Scene 3

*Enter **Bassanio** with **Shylock** the Jew.*

Shylock

Three thousand ducats,° well.[1]   *Venetian gold coins*

Bassanio

Ay, sir, for three months.

Shylock

For three months, well.

Bassanio

For the which, as I told you, Antonio shall be bound.[2]

Shylock

Antonio shall become bound, well.   5

Bassanio

May you stead° me? Will you pleasure° me? Shall I   *help / gratify*
know your answer?

Shylock

Three thousand ducats for three months, and Antonio
bound?

Bassanio

Your answer to that?   10

Shylock

Antonio is a good man.

Bassanio

Have you heard any imputation to the contrary?

Shylock

Ho, no, no, no, no. My meaning in saying he is a good
man is to have you understand me that he is sufficient.[3]
Yet his means are in supposition.[4] He hath an argosy   15
bound to Tripoli,[5] another to the Indies. I understand
moreover, upon the Rialto,[6] he hath a third at Mexico,
a fourth for England, and other ventures he hath
squandered° abroad. But ships are but boards,   *scattered*

1   *pirates*

Both Q and F print this as "Pyrats,"
perhaps suggesting a play on *land
rats* and *water rats*.

2   *bethink me*

Figure out

3   *the habitation which your prophet the
Nazarite conjured the devil into*

An allusion to the biblical story in
which Jesus (*the Nazarite*) drives
devils out of a pair of madmen
and into a herd of swine (Matthew
8:28–34)

4   *fawning publican*

I.e., cringing tax collector. The
image comes from Luke 18:9–14,
where the humility of the *publican* is
compared with the arrogance of the
Pharisee.

5   *in low simplicity / He lends out money
gratis and brings down / The rate of
usance here with us in Venice*

Out of humble foolishness he lends
money without charging interest,
forcing us (i.e., the money lenders)
in Venice to lower our interest
rates.

6   *upon the hip*

At a disadvantage (a wrestling term)

sailors but men. There be land rats and water rats,   20
water thieves and land thieves—I mean pirates¹—
and then there is the peril of waters, winds, and
rocks. The man is, notwithstanding, sufficient.
Three thousand ducats—I think I may take his
bond.   25

Bassanio

Be assured you may.

Shylock

I will be assured I may, and that I may be assured,
I will bethink me.² May I speak with Antonio?

Bassanio

If it please you to dine with us.

Shylock

Yes, to smell pork, to eat of the habitation which your   30
prophet the Nazarite conjured the devil into.³ I will
buy with you, sell with you, talk with you, walk with
forth   you, and so following,° but I will not eat with you,
drink with you, nor pray with you. What news on the
Rialto? Who is he comes here?   35

                    Enter **Antonio**.

Bassanio

This is Signior Antonio.

Shylock

[*aside*] How like a fawning publican⁴ he looks!
I hate him for he is a Christian,
But more for that in low simplicity
He lends out money gratis and brings down   40
The rate of usance here with us in Venice.⁵
If I can catch him once upon the hip,⁶
to full satisfaction   I will feed fat° the ancient grudge I bear him.

1   *our sacred nation*

I.e., the Jewish people

2   *I am debating of my present store*

**I am calculating how much cash I
have on hand.**

3   *Your worship was the last man in our
mouths.*

I.e., we were just talking about you.

4   *ye would*

You want

5   *hear you*

Listen

6   *Methoughts*

I thought

speaks abusively He hates our sacred nation,[1] and he rails,°

Even there where merchants most do congregate,   45

profit On me, my bargains, and my well-won thrift,°

Which he calls "interest." Cursèd be my tribe

If I forgive him.

Bassanio

              Shylock, do you hear?

Shylock

I am debating of my present store,[2]

And, by the near guess of my memory,   50

total I cannot instantly raise up the gross°

Of full three thousand ducats. What of that?

Tubal, a wealthy Hebrew of my tribe,

wait / months credit Will furnish me. But soft!° How many months°

Do you desire? [*to* **Antonio**] Rest you fair, good signior.   55

Your worship was the last man in our mouths.[3]

Antonio

although Shylock, albeit° I neither lend nor borrow

i.e., interest By taking nor by giving of excess,°

urgent Yet to supply the ripe° wants of my friend,

informed I'll break a custom. [*to* **Bassanio**] Is he yet possessed°   60

How much ye would?[4]

Shylock

              Ay, ay, three thousand ducats.

Antonio

And for three months.

Shylock

I had forgot—three months. [*to* **Bassanio**] You told
    me so.

[*to* **Antonio**] Well then, your bond, and, let me see—
    but hear you:[5]

Methoughts[6] you said you neither lend nor borrow   65

interest Upon advantage.°

1   *I do never use it.*

It is not my usual practice (but with *use it* punning on the meaning "engage in usury").

2   *When Jacob grazed his uncle Laban's sheep*

In Genesis 30, Jacob worked as a shepherd for Laban for seven years in order to marry Laban's daughter Rachel. When the seven years were completed, Laban permitted Jacob to keep any multicolored lambs born to the flock. Jacob placed spotted sticks in front of the breeding ewes, thus increasing the number of spotted offspring and growing quite wealthy in the process. Shylock uses this story as a biblical justification for charging interest on loans.

3   *As his wise mother wrought in his behalf, / The third possessor*

Jacob's mother Rebecca helped Jacob trick his father Isaac into giving him his brother Esau's inheritance, so Jacob became the *third* heir of his family after Abraham and Isaac (see Genesis 27).

4   *Should fall as Jacob's hire*

Should be Jacob's wages

5   *peeled me certain wands*

Peeled the bark off some sticks (*me* is a colloquial use, corresponding to the Latin ethical dative, calling attention to the speaker).

6   *deed of kind*

Natural act (of mating)

7   *a venture, sir, that Jacob served for*

A gamble that Jacob was willing to take

8   *Was this inserted to make interest good?*

Did you bring this up to prove that the taking of interest is justifiable?

Antonio

          I do never use it.[1]

Shylock

When Jacob grazed his uncle Laban's sheep[2]—

i.e., Abraham   This Jacob from our holy Abram° was,

As his wise mother wrought in his behalf,

The third possessor,[3] ay, he was the third—   70

Antonio

And what of him? Did he take interest?

Shylock

No, not take interest—not, as you would say,

Note   Directly interest. Mark° what Jacob did:

in agreement   When Laban and himself were compromised°

lambs / multicolored   That all the eanlings° which were streaked and pied°   75

in heat   Should fall as Jacob's hire,[4] the ewes, being rank,°

In end of autumn turnèd to the rams.

copulation   And, when the work of generation° was

Between these woolly breeders in the act,

The skillful shepherd peeled me certain wands.[5]   80

And in the doing of the deed of kind[6]

lustful; pregnant   He stuck them up before the fulsome° ewes,

lambing   Who, then conceiving, did in eaning° time

Give birth to   Fall° parti-colored lambs—and those were Jacob's.

This was a way to thrive, and he was blessed.   85

profit   And thrift° is blessing, if men steal it not.

Antonio

This was a venture, sir, that Jacob served for[7]—

A thing not in his power to bring to pass

But swayed and fashioned by the hand of Heaven.

Was this inserted to make interest good?[8]   90

Or is your gold and silver ewes and rams?

Shylock

I cannot tell; I make it breed as fast.

1   *holy witness*

     Biblical precedent

2   *goodly outside falsehood hath*

     **This sentiment is both proverbial
     and a theme of the play ("The world
     is still deceived with ornament").
     But see also the popular travel-
     writer Thomas Coryat (1611): "I
     observed some few of these Jews,
     especially some of the Levantines,
     to be such goodly and proper men
     that then I said to myself our Eng-
     lish proverb 'To look like a Jew'—
     whereby is meant sometimes a
     weather-beaten, warp-faced fellow,
     sometimes a frenetic and lunatic
     person, sometimes one discon-
     tented—is not true. For indeed I
     noted some of them to be most
     elegant and sweet-featured
     persons, which gave me occasion
     the more to lament their religion"
     (excerpted in Leah Marcus ed., p.
     117; see For Further Reading).**

3   *shall we be beholding to you*

     I.e., will you lend us the money?

4   *For suff'rance is the badge of all
     our tribe*

     **For patient endurance is the mark
     of the Jewish people**

5   *gaberdine*

     Long outer cloak or robe

6   *all for use of that which is mine own*

     **All because of what I do with my
     own money**

7   *Go to*

     **An expression of impatience, pro-
     test, or contempt**

8   *void your rheum*

     Spit your phlegm

9   *bondman's key*

     Slave's voice

But note me, signior—

Antonio

Observe   Mark° you this, Bassanio:

The devil can cite Scripture for his purpose.

An evil soul producing holy witness[1]   95

Is like a villain with a smiling cheek,

A goodly apple rotten at the heart.

Oh, what a goodly outside falsehood hath![2]

Shylock

Three thousand ducats—'tis a good round sum.

interest rate Three months from twelve, then. Let me see the rate°— 100

Antonio

Well, Shylock, shall we be beholding to you?[3]

Shylock

Signior Antonio, many a time and oft

berated   In the Rialto you have rated° me

lending rates   About my moneys and my usances.°

Always   Still° have I borne it with a patient shrug,   105

For suff'rance is the badge of all our tribe.[4]

You call me misbeliever, cutthroat dog,

And spit upon my Jewish gaberdine[5]—

And all for use of that which is mine own.[6]

Well then, it now appears you need my help.   110

Go to,[7] then! You come to me and you say,

"Shylock, we would have moneys." You say so—

You, that did void your rheum[8] upon my beard

kick/dog   And foot° me as you spurn a stranger cur°

goal   Over your threshold. Moneys is your suit.°   115

What should I say to you? Should I not say,

"Hath a dog money? Is it possible

A cur can lend three thousand ducats?" Or

Shall I bend low and, in a bondman's key,[9]

restrained; held in With bated° breath and whisp'ring humbleness   120

1   *for when did friendship take / A breed for barren metal of his friend*

"When did a friend ever take interest from another friend?" Antonio argues that it is unnatural for *barren metal* (infertile coins) to breed (produce offspring; i.e., more money from interest).

2   *doit*

I.e., bit (a *doit* was a Dutch coin [*duit*] worth less than a penny)

3   *kind*

Benevolent; generous (but punning on other darker senses, as with *kindness* in line 138, "according to one's natural inclination" or possibly "of the same quality as that received," as in the expression to pay someone back "in kind")

4   *single bond*

A guarantee signed by one person (i.e., Antonio) obligating himself or his heirs to repay a debt

5   *let the forfeit / Be nominated for*

Let the penalty for default be defined as

Say this: "Fair sir, you spat on me on Wednesday last;
You spurned me such a day; another time
You called me 'dog'—and for these courtesies
I'll lend you thus much moneys."

Antonio

likely I am as like° to call thee so again, 125
To spit on thee again, to spurn thee too.
If thou wilt lend this money, lend it not
As if As° to thy friends, for when did friendship take
A breed for barren metal of his friend?[1]
But lend it rather to thine enemy, 130
fail to repay Who, if he break,° thou mayst with better face
Exact the penalty.

Shylock

rage   Why, look you how you storm!°
I would be friends with you and have your love,
Forget the shames that you have stained me with,
Supply your present wants and take no doit[2] 135
interest Of usance° for my moneys—and you'll not hear me!
This is kind[3] I offer.

Bassanio

would be   This were° kindness.

Shylock

This kindness will I show.
Go with me to a notary, seal me there
Your single bond,[4] and—in a merry sport— 140
If you repay me not on such a day,
In such a place, such sum or sums as are
Expressed in the condition, let the forfeit
exact Be nominated for[5] an equal° pound
Of your fair flesh, to be cut off and taken 145
From In° what part of your body pleaseth me.

1   *dwell in my necessity*

     Remain in my need (of money)

2   *Father Abram*

     Abram (or Abraham) is the patriarch
     of the Jewish faith. See Genesis
     17:5–6: "Neither shall thy name
     anymore be called Abram, but thy
     name shall be Abraham, for a father
     of many nations have I made thee."
     (See also line 68 above.)

3   *break his day*

     Fail to pay on time

Antonio

agree   Content. In faith, I'll seal° to such a bond

And say there is much kindness in the Jew.

Bassanio

You shall not seal to such a bond for me!

I'll rather dwell in my necessity.[1]   150

Antonio

Why, fear not, man. I will not forfeit it.

Within these two months—that's a month before

This bond expires—I do expect return

Of thrice three times the value of this bond.

Shylock

O Father Abram,[2] what these Christians are,   155

i.e., to suspect   Whose own hard dealings teaches them suspect°

The thoughts of others! Pray you, tell me this:

If he should break his day,[3] what should I gain

By the exaction of the forfeiture?

A pound of man's flesh taken from a man   160

valuable   Is not so estimable,° profitable neither,

sheep / cattle   As flesh of muttons,° beefs,° or goats. I say

To buy his favor I extend this friendship.

so be it   If he will take it, so.° If not, adieu.

And for my love I pray you wrong me not.   165

Antonio

Yes, Shylock, I will seal unto this bond.

Shylock

at once   Then meet me forthwith° at the notary's.

Give him direction for this merry bond,

straightaway   And I will go and purse the ducats straight,°

unreliable   See to my house—left in the fearful° guard   170

Of an unthrifty knave—and presently

I'll be with you.

1 *gentle*

Benevolent (but with a play
on "gentile," i.e., Christian, as
throughout)

Antonio

Hurry   Hie° thee, gentle° Jew.

                                              [**Shylock**] *exits.*

The Hebrew will turn Christian. He grows kind.

Bassanio

I like not fair terms and a villain's mind.

Antonio

Come on. In this there can be no dismay.   175

due date My ships come home a month before the day.°

                                              They exit.

1   tawny Moor

    Brown (i.e., a light-skinned northern African as opposed to a darker skinned sub-Saharan African, often known as a "blacka-moor")

2   accordingly

    i.e., Dressed in the same manner

3   *shadowed livery*

    Dark servant's uniform (i.e., dark skin)

4   *To whom I am a neighbor and near bred*

    To which I was raised in close proximity (being from near the Equator) and to whom I am closely related

5   *Phoebus' fire*

    The heat of the sun. Phoebus, or Apollo, is the Roman god of the sun.

6   *reddest*

    Red blood was considered a mark of courage and virility.

7   *In terms of choice I am not solely led / By nice direction of a maiden's eyes.*

    i.e., in choosing I am not swayed by physical appearance (*nice direction* meaning "discriminating guidance." Portia's choice will not be influenced either by the guidance of her own eyes, or by the recommendations of the *best regarded virgins* of Morocco.)

8   *lott'ry of my destiny*

    Portia's fate is a lottery because it is out of her control; she can only marry the man who chooses the correct chest.

9   *hedged me by his wit*

    Confined me in his wisdom

10 *stood as fair*

    Would seem as attractive as

11 *caskets*

    Shakespeare's use of the casket story, which has its roots in ancient myth, derives most immediately from Richard Robinson's 1571 translation of the *Gesta Romanorum*. In the Thirty-second History, a princess seeking to marry the son of the emperor of Rome must pass a test. The emperor sets before her three caskets: The gold one bears the inscription "Whoso chooseth me shall find that he deserveth"; the silver one reads "Whoso chooseth me shall find that his nature desireth;" and the lead, "Whoso chooseth me, shall find that God hath disposed for him." The first contains bones, the second worms, and the third precious jewels. The princess, of course, chooses the last one and marries the prince.

Act 2, Scene 1

Enter [the Prince of] **Morocco,** *a tawny Moor[1] all in white, and three or four followers accordingly,[2] with* **Portia, Nerissa,** *and their train.°*

attendants

Morocco

Dislike Mislike° me not for my complexion,
bright The shadowed livery[3] of the burnished° sun,
To whom I am a neighbor and near bred.[4]
Bring me the fairest creature northward born,
Where Phoebus' fire[5] scarce thaws the icicles,   5
And let us make incision for your love
To prove whose blood is reddest,[6] his or mine.
appearance I tell thee, lady, this aspect° of mine
frightened Hath feared° the valiant. By my love I swear
climate (i.e., region) The best-regarded virgins of our clime°   10
Have loved it too. I would not change this hue
Except to steal your thoughts, my gentle queen.

Portia

In terms of choice I am not solely led
By nice direction of a maiden's eyes.[7]
Besides, the lott'ry of my destiny[8]   15
Denies Bars° me the right of voluntary choosing.
limited But if my father had not scanted° me
And hedged me by his wit[9] to yield myself
His wife who wins me by that means I told you,
Yourself, renownèd Prince, then stood as fair[10]   20
visitor As any comer° I have looked on yet
For my affection.

Morocco

               Even for that I thank you.
Therefore I pray you lead me to the caskets[11]
carved sword To try my fortune. By this scimitar°

1   *That won three fields of Sultan Solyman*

Who had in three battles defeated
the Turkish leader Suleiman.
(Suleiman the Magnificent ruled as
sultan of the Ottoman Empire from
1520 to 1566. The Ottoman Empire
was the most powerful empire
in the world in the 16th and 17th
centuries and remained powerful
well into the 19th century.)

2   *If Hercules and Lychas play at dice / Which*
is the better man, the greater throw / May
turn by fortune from the weaker hand.

If *Hercules* (the famous Greek hero)
and *Lychas* (his servant) were to
roll dice to determine who was the
worthier, it would be possible for
the lesser man to win by luck.

3   *Nor will not.*

I will not (propose to any other
woman).

Emperor of Persia That slew the Sophy° and a Persian prince   25
　　　　　　　　That won three fields of Sultan Solyman,[1]
outstare I would o'erstare° the sternest eyes that look,
　　　　　　　　Outbrave the heart most daring on the earth,
　　　　　　　　Pluck the young sucking cubs from the she-bear,
he Yea, mock the lion when 'a° roars for prey,   30
　　　　　　　　To win the lady. But alas the while!
　　　　　　　　If Hercules and Lychas play at dice
　　　　　　　　Which is the better man, the greater throw
　　　　　　　　May turn by fortune from the weaker hand.[2]
i.e., Hercules So is Alcides° beaten by his page,   35
　　　　　　　　And so may I, blind fortune leading me,
　　　　　　　　Miss that which one unworthier may attain
　　　　　　　　And die with grieving.

Portia
　　　　　　　　　　　　You must take your chance,
　　　　　　　　And either not attempt to choose at all
　　　　　　　　Or swear before you choose, if you choose wrong,   40
any woman Never to speak to lady° afterward
warned In way of marriage. Therefore be advised.°

Morocco
Nor will not.[3] Come; bring me unto my chance.

Portia
First, forward to the temple. After dinner
Your hazard shall be made.

Morocco
　　　　　　　　　　　　Good fortune then,   45
To make me blessed or cursèd'st among men.

　　　　　　　　　　　　　　　　They exit.

1 *The fiend is at mine elbow and tempts me*

Launcelot imagines a devil (*fiend*) whispering in one ear, urging him to run away from Shylock; his *conscience*, at the other, admonishes him to stay with his master.

2 *take the start*

Get going

3 Fia!

I.e., get away (from the Italian *via*)

4 *For the heavens*

A mild oath, "before the heavens"

5 *my father did something smack*

(1) my father did somewhat taste of; (2) my father did kiss something (This and the following phrases all are Launcelot's failed efforts to say something about his father's sexual appetite.)

6 *something grow to*

Somewhat enlarge

7 *he had a kind of taste*

He had some inclination

8 *God bless the mark*

I.e., God forgive me.

9 *saving your reverence*

Begging your pardon

10 *incarnation*

I.e., incarnate (literally, embodied in flesh). Launcelot's speech is filled with *malapropisms* (comic misuses of words, usually results of having confused the intended word with a similar sounding one). The *incarnation* is the birth of Jesus understood as God embodied in the flesh.

Act 2, Scene 2

*Enter [**Launcelot**] the clown, alone.*

Launcelot

allow Certainly my conscience will serve° me to run from this
Jew, my master. The fiend is at mine elbow and tempts
me,¹ saying to me, "Gobbo," "Launcelot Gobbo," "Good
Launcelot," or "Good Gobbo," or "Good Launcelot
Gobbo"—"use your legs, take the start,² run away." My   5
caution conscience says, "No. Take heed,° honest Launcelot.
Take heed, honest Gobbo," or, as aforesaid, "Honest
Launcelot Gobbo, do not run. Scorn running with thy
depart heels." Well, the most courageous fiend bids me pack.°
"*Fia!*"³ says the fiend. "Away!" says the fiend. "For   10
the heavens,⁴ rouse up a brave mind," says the fiend,
"and run." Well, my conscience, hanging about the
neck of my heart, says very wisely to me, "My honest
friend Launcelot, being an honest man's son"—or
rather an honest woman's son, for indeed my father   15
did something smack⁵—something grow to⁶—he had
a kind of taste⁷—well, my conscience says, "Launcelot,
budge not." "Budge!" says the fiend. "Budge not," says
my conscience. "Conscience," say I, "you counsel well."
"Fiend," say I, "you counsel well." To be ruled by my   20
conscience I should stay with the Jew my master, who,
God bless the mark,⁸ is a kind of devil. And to run away
from the Jew I should be ruled by the fiend, who, saving
your reverence,⁹ is the devil himself. Certainly the Jew
is the very devil incarnation.¹⁰ And, in my conscience,   25
my conscience is but a kind of hard conscience, to offer
to counsel me to stay with the Jew. The fiend gives the
more friendly counsel. I will run, fiend. My heels are at
your commandment. I will run.

1   *high-gravel blind*

Launcelot invents a new category
of blindness: *high-gravel blind*
would be the midpoint between
partial blindness (*sand-blind*)
and total blindness (*stone-blind*).

2   *try confusions*

"Try conclusions" was an
idiom meaning "experiment," but
Launcelot's characteristic mistake
has its own unintended logic, as his
speech to his father reveals.

3   *Marry*

Indeed; to be sure (a mild oath
derived from "by the Virgin Mary")

4   *raise the waters*

I.e., cause him to cry

Enter old **Gobbo** *with a basket.*

Gobbo

Master young man, you, I pray you, which is the way 30
to Master Jew's?

Launcelot

[*aside*] O heavens, this is my true-begotten father, who,
being more than sand-blind—high-gravel blind[1]—
knows me not. I will try confusions[2] with him.

Gobbo

Master young gentleman, I pray you, which is the way 35
to Master Jew's?

Launcelot

Turn up on your right hand at the next turning, but
at the next turning of all on your left. Marry,[3] at the
very next turning, turn of no hand, but turn down
indirectly to the Jew's house. 40

Gobbo

i.e., saints By God's sonties,° 'twill be a hard way to hit. Can you
tell me whether one Launcelot that dwells with him
dwell with him or no?

Launcelot

Talk you of young Master Launcelot? [*aside*] Mark me
now. Now will I raise the waters.[4]—Talk you of young 45
Master Launcelot?

Gobbo

No "Master," sir, but a poor man's son. His father,
exceedingly though I say 't, is an honest exceeding° poor man and,
well-to-do God be thanked, well-to-live.°

Launcelot

he Well, let his father be what 'a° will, we talk of young 50
Master Launcelot.

1   *father*

A polite form of address to an old man

2   *Sisters Three*

The *fates* or *destinies*, the three sister deities of classical mythology who controlled human life spans

3   *the very staff of my age*

My strongest support in my old age

4   *hovel-post*

Support beam

5   *fail of the knowing me*

(Still) not be able to recognize me

Gobbo

Your worship's friend and Launcelot, sir.

Launcelot

therefore (Latin) But I pray you, *ergo*,° old man, *ergo*, I beseech you, talk
you of young Master Launcelot?

Gobbo

if Of Launcelot, an° 't please your mastership.   55

Launcelot

Ergo, Master Launcelot. Talk not of Master Launcelot,
father,¹ for the young gentleman, according to fates
and destinies and such odd sayings, the Sisters Three²
and such branches of learning, is indeed deceased, or,
as you would say in plain terms, gone to Heaven.   60

Gobbo

Marry, God forbid! The boy was the very staff of my
age,³ my very prop.

Launcelot

club Do I look like a cudgel° or a hovel-post,⁴ a staff or a
prop? Do you know me, father?

Gobbo

Alack the day, I know you not, young gentleman. But I   65
pray you, tell me, is my boy, God rest his soul, alive or
dead?

Launcelot

Do you not know me, father?

Gobbo

Alack, sir, I am sand-blind. I know you not.

Launcelot

Nay, indeed if you had your eyes, you might fail of the   70
knowing me.⁵ It is a wise father that knows his own
child. Well, old man, I will tell you news of your son.
Give me your blessing. Truth will come to light.

[*He kneels.*]

1   *grows backward*

     I.e., gets shorter as it grows

2   *set up my rest*

     Made up my mind

Murder cannot be hid long—a man's son may, but in
the end truth will out.   75

Gobbo

Pray you, sir, stand up. I am sure you are not Launcelot
my boy.

Launcelot

Pray you, let's have no more fooling about it, but give
me your blessing. I am Launcelot, your boy that was,
your son that is, your child that shall be.   80

Gobbo

believe   I cannot think° you are my son.

Launcelot

I know not what I shall think of that, but I am Launcelot,
servant   the Jew's man,° and I am sure Margery your wife is my
mother.

Gobbo

Her name is Margery, indeed. I'll be sworn, if thou be   85
Launcelot, thou art mine own flesh and blood. [*feels the
back of* **Launcelot***'s head*] Lord worshipped might he be,
what a beard hast thou got! Thou hast got more hair on
cart horse   thy chin than Dobbin my fill-horse° has on his tail.

Launcelot

[*standing*] It should seem then that Dobbin's tail grows   90
on   backward.¹ I am sure he had more hair of° his tail than
I have of my face when I last saw him.

Gobbo

Lord, how art thou changed! How dost thou and thy
get along   master agree?° I have brought him a present. How
'gree you now?   95

Launcelot

Well, well, but for mine own part, as I have set up my
rest² to run away, so I will not rest till I have run some
distance / absolute   ground.° My master's a very° Jew. Give him a present?

1 *Give me*

I.e., give (*me* is a colloquial form calling attention to the speaker)

2 *as far as God has any ground*

I.e., to the end of the Earth

3 *liveries to making*

Servants to the preparation

4 *Gramercy!*

Many thanks

5 *infection*

I.e., affection; inclination (Gobbo, like his son, uses many malapropisms)

noose   a present? Give him a halter!° I am famished in his
count   service. You may tell° every finger I have with my ribs.   100
   Father, I am glad you are come. Give me¹ your present
splendid   to one Master Bassanio, who indeed gives rare° new
uniforms   liveries.° If I serve not him, I will run as far as God
excellent   has any ground.²—O rare° fortune! Here comes the
Go to   man.—To° him, Father, for I am a Jew if I serve the Jew   105
   any longer.

        Enter **Bassanio** *with [***Leonardo*** and] a follower
        or two.*

Bassanio
hurried   [*to a follower*] You may do so, but let it be so hasted° that
latest   supper be ready at the farthest° by five of the clock. See
   these letters delivered, put the liveries to making,³ and
ask/at once   desire° Gratiano to come anon° to my lodging.   110
                              [*Follower exits.*]

Launcelot
To him, Father.

Gobbo
[*to* **Bassanio**] God bless your worship!

Bassanio
anything   Gramercy.⁴ Wouldst thou aught° with me?

Gobbo
Here's my son, sir, a poor boy—

Launcelot
Not a poor boy, sir, but the rich Jew's man that would,   115
sir, as my father shall specify—

Gobbo
He hath a great infection,⁵ sir, as one would say, to
serve—

1   *scarce cater-cousins*

    I.e., hardly close friends

2   *preferment*

    Advancement; promotion

3   *The old proverb*

    I.e., "the grace of God is gear
    (possession) enough."

Launcelot

Indeed, the short and the long is, I serve the Jew and
have a desire, as my father shall specify— 120

Gobbo

His master and he, saving your worship's reverence,
are scarce cater-cousins[1]—

Launcelot

To be brief, the very truth is that the Jew, having done
me wrong, doth cause me, as my father, being, I hope,
an old man, shall frutify° unto you— 125

i.e., certify

Gobbo

I have here a dish of doves that I would bestow upon
your worship, and my suit is—

Launcelot

In very brief, the suit is impertinent° to myself, as your
worship shall know by this honest old man—and though
I say it, though old man, yet poor man, my father— 130

i.e., pertinent

Bassanio

One speak for both. What would° you?

wish

Launcelot

Serve you, sir.

Gobbo

That is the very defect° of the matter, sir.

i.e., effect

Bassanio

[*to* **Launcelot**] I know thee well. Thou hast obtained
thy suit.
Shylock thy master spoke with me this day, 135
And hath preferred° thee, if it be preferment[2]
To leave a rich Jew's service to become
The follower of so poor a gentleman.

recommended

Launcelot

The old proverb[3] is very well parted° between my
master Shylock and you, sir—you have "the grace of 140

divided

1 *table*

   Palm of the hand

2 *Go to.*

   An expression of impatience

3 *simple coming-in*

   **Nice beginning (probably also with
   a sexual sense)**

4 *be in peril of my life with the edge of a*

   feather-bed

   **Have a disastrous marriage
   (Launcelot continues to read his
   fortune in his palm)**

God," sir, and he hath "enough."

Bassanio

Thou speak'st it well.—Go, father, with thy son.

—Take leave of thy old master and inquire

uniform — My lodging out.—[*to followers*] Give him a livery°

decorated with braid — More guarded° than his fellows'. See it done.   145

Launcelot

job as a servant — Father, in. I cannot get a service,° no. I have ne'er a
tongue in my head. [*reading his own palm*] Well, if any
man in Italy have a fairer table¹ which doth offer to
swear upon a book, I shall have good fortune. Go to.²

unremarkable — Here's a simple° line of life. Here's a small trifle of   150
wives. Alas, fifteen wives is nothing! Eleven widows
and nine maids is a simple coming-in³ for one man.
And then to 'scape drowning thrice and to be in peril of
my life with the edge of a feather-bed.⁴ Here are simple

escapes; escapades — 'scapes.° Well, if Fortune be a woman, she's a good   155

business — wench for this gear. °—Father, come. I'll take my leave

i.e., instant — of the Jew in the twinkling.°

                    [**Launcelot** *the*] *clown* [*and old* **Gobbo**] *exit.*

Bassanio

I pray thee, good Leonardo, think on this.
[*hands him a paper*] These things being bought and

i.e., stored on ship —   orderly bestowed,°

Return in haste, for I do feast tonight   160

Hurry — My best esteemed acquaintance. Hie° thee; go.

Leonardo

My best endeavors shall be done herein.

                    Enter **Gratiano**.

Gratiano

[*to* **Leonardo**] Where is your master?

1   *bold of voice*

    Outspoken

2   *misconst'red*

    Misconstrued; misunderstood

3   *sober habit*

    Serious manner

4   *Wear prayer books*

    **Carry prayer books (to appear
    religious)**

5   *while grace is saying, hood mine eyes /
    Thus with my hat*

    **While grace is being said, take off
    my hat and cover my eyes with it (to
    demonstrate my piety)**

6   *Use all the observance of civility*

    Observe proper decorum

7   *sad ostent*

    Solemn or serious appearance

Leonardo

> Yonder, sir, he walks.

> **Leonardo** *exits.*

Gratiano

Signior Bassanio!

Bassanio

Gratiano! 165

Gratiano

a request　I have suit° to you.

Bassanio

> You have obtained it.

Gratiano

You must not deny me. I must go with you to Belmont.

Bassanio

Why, then you must. But hear thee, Gratiano,
Thou art too wild, too rude and bold of voice [1]—
Qualities　Parts° that become thee happily enough 170
And in such eyes as ours appear not faults.
appear　But where thou art not known, why, there they show°
unrestrained　Something too liberal.° Pray thee, take pain
moderate　To allay° with some cold drops of modesty
impetuous　Thy skipping° spirit, lest through thy wild behavior 175
I be misconst'red [2] in the place I go to
And lose my hopes.

Gratiano

> Signior Bassanio, hear me.

If I do not put on a sober habit, [3]
Talk with respect and swear but now and then,
Wear prayer books [4] in my pocket, look demurely— 180
Nay more, while grace is saying, hood mine eyes
Thus with my hat, [5] and sigh and say, "Amen"—
Use all the observance of civility [6]
Like one well studied in a sad ostent [7]

1   *boldest suit of mirth*

Most extravagant party clothes (as
opposed to the *sober habit* Gratiano
promises to wear in Belmont
(line 178)

grandmother   To please his grandam,° never trust me more.   185

Bassanio

behavior   Well, we shall see your bearing.°

Gratiano

exclude / judge   Nay, but I bar° tonight. You shall not gauge° me
By what we do tonight.

Bassanio

would be a   No, that were° pity.
I would entreat you rather to put on
Your boldest suit of mirth,¹ for we have friends   190
intend   That purpose° merriment; but fare you well.
I have some business.

Gratiano

And I must to Lorenzo and the rest,
But we will visit you at suppertime.   *They exit.*

1   *play the knave and get thee*

    I.e., manage to deceive (Shylock)
    and marry you

2   *this strife*

    I.e., her divided feelings

Act 2, Scene 3

Enter **Jessica** *and* [**Launcelot**] *the clown.*

Jessica
I am sorry thou wilt leave my father so.
Our house is Hell, and thou, a merry devil,
Didst rob it of some taste of tediousness.
But fare thee well; [*handing him a coin*] there is a ducat
    for thee.
And Launcelot, soon at supper shalt thou see   5
Lorenzo, who is thy new master's guest.
Give him this letter. Do it secretly.
And so farewell. I would not have my father
See me in talk with thee.

Launcelot
i.e., inhibit   Adieu. Tears exhibit° my tongue, most beautiful pagan,   10
most sweet Jew! If a Christian do not play the knave and
get thee,¹ I am much deceived. But adieu. These foolish
somewhat   drops do something° drown my manly spirit. Adieu.

Jessica
Farewell, good Launcelot.   [**Launcelot** *exits.*]
Alack, what heinous sin is it in me   15
To be ashamed to be my father's child?
But though I am a daughter to his blood,
behavior   I am not to his manners.° O Lorenzo,
If thou keep promise, I shall end this strife,²
Become a Christian and thy loving wife.   *She exits.*   20

1   *'Tis vile, unless it may be quaintly ordered*

     **It's a bad idea, unless it can be care-
     fully organized.**

2   *By your leave*

     **With your permission (a polite apol-
     ogy for one's departure)**

Act 2, Scene 4

Enter **Gratiano**, **Lorenzo**, **Salarino**, *and* **Solanio**.

Lorenzo

during   Nay, we will slink away in° suppertime,

ourselves   Disguise us° at my lodging, and return,

    All in an hour.

Gratiano

    We have not made good preparation.

Salarino

about   We have not spoke us yet of° torchbearers.   5

Solanio

    'Tis vile, unless it may be quaintly ordered,[1]

opinion   And better in my mind° not undertook.

Lorenzo

    'Tis now but four o'clock. We have two hours

prepare   To furnish° us.

Enter **Launcelot** *[with a letter]*.

               Friend Launcelot, what's the news?

Launcelot

If   *[handing* **Lorenzo** *the letter]* An° it shall please you to   10

open / tell you   break° up this, it shall seem to signify.°

Lorenzo

handwriting   I know the hand.° In faith, 'tis a fair hand,

is written   And whiter than the paper it writ° on

    Is the fair hand that writ.

Gratiano

               Love news, in faith?

Launcelot

[to **Lorenzo***]* By your leave,[2] sir.   15

1   *must needs*

     Have to

2   *page's suit*

     **Young man's clothing. A woman
     dressing in male clothing to escape
     her lover was a familiar convention
     in 16th- and 17th-century literature.
     See for example John Donne's "El-
     egy XVI. On His Mistress" in which
     the speaker's mistress dresses as a
     "feign'd Page" to escape with him
     from her "father's wrath" (14, 7).**

3   *gentle*

     Kind (with a pun on "gentile")

Lorenzo

Whither goest thou?

Launcelot

Marry, sir, to bid my old master the Jew to sup tonight
with my new master the Christian.

Lorenzo

[*giving* **Launcelot** *money*] Hold. Here; take this. Tell
    gentle Jessica
I will not fail her. Speak it privately; go.   20

                                    [**Launcelot**] *exits.*

—Gentlemen,

Will you prepare you for this masque tonight?

in possession I am provided° of a torchbearer.

Salarino

immediately Ay, marry, I'll be gone about it straight.°

Solanio

And so will I.

Lorenzo

                        Meet me and Gratiano   25

i.e., about an At Gratiano's lodging some° hour hence.

Salarino

'Tis good we do so.   [**Salarino** *and* **Solanio**] *exit.*

Gratiano

Was not that letter from fair Jessica?

Lorenzo

instructed I must needs¹ tell thee all. She hath directed°

How I shall take her from her father's house,   30

supplied What gold and jewels she is furnished° with,

What page's suit² she hath in readiness.

If e'er the Jew her father come to Heaven,

It will be for his gentle³ daughter's sake;

path And never dare misfortune cross her foot°   35

1 *never dare misfortune cross her foot /*
Unless she do it under this excuse: / That
she is issue to a faithless Jew

**I.e., Jessica will never be troubled
by misfortune, unless misfortune
blame her for being the daughter
of a Jew.**

i.e., misfortune   Unless she° do it under this excuse:

i.e., Jessica   That she° is issue to a faithless Jew. **¹**

Come; go with me. [*gives* **Gratiano** *the letter*] Peruse this
as thou goest.

Fair Jessica shall be my torchbearer.   [*They*] *exit.*

1 *his man that was*

His former servant

2 *rend apparel out*

Wear out your clothes

3 *bid for*

Invited out of

4 *right loath*

Very reluctant

5 *There is some ill a-brewing towards my rest*

There is some misfortune looming that will disturb my peace of mind.

Act 2, Scene 5

*Enter [**Shylock** the] Jew and [**Launcelot**,] his man that was,* [1]
the clown.

Shylock

Well, thou shalt see (thy eyes shall be thy judge)

between The difference of° old Shylock and Bassanio.

overeat —What, Jessica!—Thou shalt not gormandize°

As thou hast done with me.—What, Jessica!

—And sleep and snore, and rend apparel out.[2]   5

—Why, Jessica, I say!

Launcelot

Why, Jessica!

Shylock

asks Who bids° thee call? I do not bid thee call.

Launcelot

accustomed Your worship was wont° to tell me I could do nothing
without bidding.

Enter **Jessica.**

Jessica

Call you? What is your will?   10

Shylock

I am bid forth to supper, Jessica.

why There are my keys.—But wherefore° should I go?

I am not bid for[3] love. They flatter me;

But yet I'll go in hate to feed upon

wasteful The prodigal° Christian.—Jessica, my girl,   15

Look to my house. I am right loath[4] to go.

There is some ill a-brewing towards my rest,[5]

last night For I did dream of money bags tonight.°

115

1   *my nose fell a-bleeding*

A nosebleed was considered a bad omen. Here, Launcelot mocks Shylock's superstitious dream.

2   *Black Monday*

Easter Monday. The rest of Launcelot's speech is nonsense.

3   *wry-necked fife*

Crooked-necked fife player (a reference to the fact that a musician has to turn his head sideways to play the fife, a small flute-like instrument)

4   *varnished faces*

Painted masks

5   *By Jacob's staff*

An invented Jewish oath; Jacob, one of the Old Testament patriarchs, left home carrying only a staff and returned very wealthy. See Genesis 32:10.

6   *I have no mind of feasting forth tonight*

I do not wish to dine out tonight.

7   *sirrah*

A term of address normally used for social inferiors

8   *for all this*

Despite all this (admonishment from Shylock)

9   *fool of Hagar's offspring*

I.e., fool of a gentile (a non-Jew, a Christian). In the Old Testament (Genesis 16), the Egyptian servant Hagar bore Abraham a son whom she named Ishmael. Hagar and Ishmael were both expelled from the household after Sarah, Abraham's wife, gave birth to a son of her own.

Launcelot

I beseech you, sir, go. My young master doth expect

i.e., approach   your reproach.°   20

Shylock

So do I his.

Launcelot

And they have conspired together. I will not say you

masked ball   shall see a masque,° but if you do then it was not for

nothing that my nose fell a-bleeding[1] on Black Mon-

day[2] last, at six o'clock i' th' morning, falling out that   25

year on Ash Wednesday was four year in th' afternoon.

Shylock

What, are there masques? Hear you me, Jessica.

Lock up my doors, and when you hear the drum

And the vile squealing of the wry-necked fife,[3]

Climb / windows   Clamber° not you up to the casements° then,   30

Nor thrust your head into the public street

To gaze on Christian fools with varnished faces,[4]

Instead   But° stop my house's ears—I mean my casements.

foolishness   Let not the sound of shallow fopp'ry° enter

My sober house. By Jacob's staff,[5] I swear,   35

I have no mind of feasting forth[6] tonight.

But I will go.—Go you before me, sirrah.[7]

Say I will come.

Launcelot

                  I will go before, sir.

—Mistress, look out at window, for all this.[8]

There will come a Christian by   40

Will be worth a Jewess' eye.   [*He exits.*]

Shylock

What says that fool of Hagar's offspring,[9] ha?

Jessica

His words were, "Farewell, mistress." Nothing else.

1   *Drones hive not with me.*

I.e., those who will not be productive cannot live with me. (*Drones* are male honey bees that do no work for the hive other than impregnating the queen.)

2   *Fast bind, fast find*

I.e., when something is securely put away, it will stay there and be easily found (a familiar proverb).

Shylock

fool	The patch° is kind enough, but a huge feeder,
i.e., anything useful	Snail-slow in profit,° and he sleeps by day 45
(a nocturnal animal)	More than the wildcat.° Drones hive not with me.[1]
	Therefore I part with him, and part with him
	To one that I would have him help to waste
	His borrowed purse. Well, Jessica, go in.
	Perhaps I will return immediately. 50
	Do as I bid you. Shut doors after you.
	Fast bind, fast find:[2]
irrelevant; worn out	A proverb never stale° in thrifty mind. *He exits.*

Jessica

thwarted	Farewell, and if my fortune be not crossed,°
	I have a father, you a daughter, lost. *She exits.* 55

1   masquers

Guests at masked balls often wore fantastic masks and elaborate costumes. See 2.4.1–7, where Gratiano, Lorenzo, Salarino, and Solanio discuss their preparation for their appearance at the ball.

2   *make stand*

Wait

3   *Oh, ten times faster Venus' pigeons fly / To seal love's bonds new made than they are wont / To keep obligèd faith unforfeited.*

The doves that draw the chariot of Venus fly ten times faster (i.e., lovers are always more eager) to establish a new love affair than to preserve a contracted marriage.

4   *ever holds*

Is always true

5   *How like a younger or a prodigal*

A reference to the biblical parable of the prodigal son, in which the younger of a man's two sons leaves home and, after squandering his inheritance, returns in destitution to his family (Luke 15:11–31).

6   *scarfèd bark*

Boat adorned with streamers

7   *native bay*

Home port

8   *overweathered ribs*

Weather-beaten timbers

Act 2, Scene 6

Enter the masquers,[1] **Gratiano** *and* **Salarino**.

Gratiano

projecting roof This is the penthouse° under which Lorenzo
Desired us to make stand.[2]

Salarino

                          His hour is almost past.

Gratiano

And it is marvel he outdwells his hour,
For lovers ever run before the clock.

Salarino

Oh, ten times faster Venus' pigeons fly   5
To seal love's bonds new made than they are wont
To keep obligèd faith unforfeited.[3]

Gratiano

That ever holds.[4] Who riseth from a feast
the same With that° keen appetite that he sits down?
retrace Where is the horse that doth untread° again   10
paces / unabated His tedious measures° with the unbated° fire
That he did pace them first? All things that are,
Are with more spirit chasèd than enjoyed.
How like a younger or a prodigal[5]
sets out The scarfèd bark[6] puts° from her native bay,[7]   15
wanton; unreliable Hugged and embracèd by the strumpet° wind.
How like the prodigal doth she return
With overweathered ribs[8] and raggèd sails,
threadbare / torn Lean,° rent,° and beggared by the strumpet wind.

Salarino

Here comes Lorenzo. More of this hereafter.   20

Enter **Lorenzo**.

1   *your patience*

    I.e., I beg your patience.

2   above

    Presumably Jessica appears in the
    gallery space above the main stage
    (see Fig. 1 on page 284).

3   *Tell me for more certainty*

    Tell me so that I can be certain (that
    you are who you claim to be).

4   *good sooth*

    In truth

5   *light*

    Obvious (with a pun on the mean-
    ing "immoral")

Lorenzo

delay   Sweet friends, your patience[1] for my long abode.°

Not I but my affairs have made you wait.

When you shall please to play the thieves for wives,

wait   I'll watch° as long for you then. Approach.

i.e., future father-in-law   Here dwells my father° Jew.—Ho! Who's within?   25

[*Enter*] **Jessica** *above,*[2] [*disguised as a boy*].

Jessica

Who are you? Tell me for more certainty,[3]

Although / voice   Albeit° I'll swear that I do know your tongue.°

Lorenzo

Lorenzo, and thy love.

Jessica

Lorenzo certain, and my love indeed—

For who love I so much? And now who knows   30

But you, Lorenzo, whether I am yours?

Lorenzo

Heaven and thy thoughts are witness that thou art.

Jessica

Here; catch this casket; it is worth the pains.

I am glad 'tis night, you do not look on me,

change (of dress)   For I am much ashamed of my exchange.°   35

But love is blind, and lovers cannot see

cunning   The pretty° follies that themselves commit,

For if they could, Cupid himself would blush

To see me thus transformèd to a boy.

Lorenzo

Descend, for you must be my torchbearer.   40

Jessica

What, must I hold a candle to my shames?

They in themselves, good sooth,[4] are too too light.[5]

1   *'tis an office of discovery*

    **It is the duty (of torchbearers) to
reveal things.**

2   *the close night doth play the runaway*

    **I.e., the concealing night is slipping
away from us.**

3   *I will make fast the doors and gild myself /
With some more ducats*

    **I will shut the doors tightly and
furnish myself with more coins.**

4   *by my hood*

    **A mild oath (swearing, perhaps, by
the *hood* of his costume)**

5   *gentle*

    **Gentlewoman, with a pun on
"gentile"**

Why, 'tis an office of discovery, [1] love,
And I should be obscured.

Lorenzo

                              So are you, sweet,

outfit   Even in the lovely garnish° of a boy.   45

But come at once,
For the close night doth play the runaway, [2]

waited   And we are stayed° for at Bassanio's feast.

Jessica

secure   I will make fast° the doors and gild myself

immediately   With some more ducats, [3] and be with you straight.°   50

                              [**Jessica** exits, *above*.]

Gratiano

Now, by my hood, [4] a gentle [5] and no Jew.

Lorenzo

Curse   Beshrew° me but I love her heartily,

For she is wise, if I can judge of her,
And fair she is, if that mine eyes be true,
And true she is, as she hath proved herself;   55
And therefore, like herself—wise, fair, and true—
Shall she be placèd in my constant soul.

Enter **Jessica**.

i.e., Jessica disguised   What, art thou come?—On, gentleman,° away!

Our masquing mates by this time for us stay.

                    [**Lorenzo** *with* **Jessica** *and* **Salarino**] *exit*.

Enter **Antonio**.

Antonio

Who's there?

1   *come about*

**Turned (so it is now in the right
direction to sail)**

Gratiano

        Signior Antonio?   60

Antonio

Fie, fie, Gratiano! Where are all the rest?

wait 'Tis nine o'clock. Our friends all stay° for you.

No masque tonight; the wind is come about.¹

Bassanio presently will go aboard.

I have sent twenty out to seek for you.   65

Gratiano

of I am glad on° 't. I desire no more delight

Than to be under sail and gone tonight.   *They exit.*

1   *all as blunt*

Just as dull

2   *shows of dross*

Appearances of worthlessness

3   *virgin hue*

I.e., pale color (*virgin* because the
moon is associated with Diana, the
goddess of chastity)

Act 2, Scene 7

*Enter **Portia** with [the Prince of] **Morocco**, and both their trains.*

Portia

reveal   [*to servant*] Go; draw aside the curtains and discover°

various   The several° caskets to this noble prince.

                              [*The curtain is drawn.*]

    [*to **Morocco***] Now make your choice.

Morocco

which   This first, of gold, who° this inscription bears:

    "Who chooseth me shall gain what many men desire."   5

    The second, silver, which this promise carries:

    "Who chooseth me shall get as much as he deserves."

    This third, dull lead, with warning all as blunt:[1]

risk   "Who chooseth me must give and hazard° all he hath."

    How shall I know if I do choose the right?   10

Portia

    The one of them contains my picture, Prince.

    If you choose that, then I am yours withal.

Morocco

    Some god direct my judgment! Let me see.

    I will survey th' inscriptions back again.

    What says this leaden casket?   15

    "Who chooseth me must give and hazard all he hath."

    Must give—for what? For lead? Hazard for lead?

    This casket threatens. Men that hazard all

    Do it in hope of fair advantages.

    A golden mind stoops not to shows of dross.[2]   20

neither/anything   I'll then nor° give nor hazard aught° for lead.

    What says the silver with her virgin hue?[3]

    "Who chooseth me shall get as much as he deserves."

1   *weigh thy value with an even hand*

     I.e., evaluate your merit impartially

2   *beest rated by thy estimation*

     Are measured by your reputation

3   *mortal breathing*

     Living

4   *Hyrcanian deserts*

     Desert area south of the Caspian
     Sea, notorious for its dangers

5   *watery kingdom*

     I.e., the sea, Neptune's *kingdom*

6   *ambitious head*

     Probably meaning only "large
     waves" but might refer to Neptune
     as the ruler (*head*) of the sea

7   *It were too gross / To rib her cerecloth*

     (Lead) would be too coarse a
     substance in which to enclose her
     burial sheet.

8   *A coin that bears the figure of an angel*

     The English gold coin called an *angel*
     was engraved with the picture of
     the archangel Michael spearing a
     dragon.

"As much as he deserves?" Pause there, Morocco,

And weigh thy value with an even hand. [1]   25

If thou beest rated by thy estimation, [2]

Thou dost deserve enough, and yet enough

May not extend so far as to the lady;

And yet to be afeard of my deserving

disparagement Were but a weak disabling° of myself.   30

As much as I deserve? Why, that's the lady.

I do in birth deserve her, and in fortunes,

In graces, and in qualities of breeding.

But more than these, in love I do deserve.

What if I strayed no farther, but chose here?   35

engraved Let's see once more this saying graved° in gold:

"Who chooseth me shall gain what many men desire."

Why, that's the lady. All the world desires her.

From the four corners of the Earth they come

To kiss this shrine, this mortal breathing[3] saint.   40

vast The Hyrcanian deserts[4] and the vasty° wilds

highways Of wide Arabia are as throughfares° now

For princes to come view fair Portia.

The watery kingdom, [5] whose ambitious head[6]

barrier Spits in the face of Heaven, is no bar°   45

To stop the foreign spirits, but they come

_As if_ As° o'er a brook to see fair Portia.

One of these three contains her heavenly picture.

likely Is 't like° that lead contains her? 'Twere damnation

To think so base a thought. It were too gross   50

dark To rib her cerecloth[7] in the obscure° grave.

confined Or shall I think in silver she's immured, °

purified Being ten times undervalued to tried° gold?

O sinful thought! Never so rich a gem

anything less Was set in worse° than gold. They have in England   55

A coin that bears the figure of an angel[8]

1   *carrion death*

    Rotting skull

2   *inscrolled*

    Written on a scroll

3   *complexion*

    (1) color; (2) temperament

engraved   Stamped in gold, but that's insculped° upon.

But here an angel in a golden bed

Lies all within.—Deliver me the key.

Here do I choose, and thrive I as I may.   60

Portia

image   There, take it, Prince. And if my form° lie there

Then I am yours.

[**Morocco** _is handed a key and opens the casket._]

Morocco

O Hell, what have we here?

A carrion death,[1] within whose empty eye

There is a written scroll. I'll read the writing:

glitters   [_reads_] "All that glisters° is not gold;   65

Often have you heard that told.

Many a man his life hath sold

Only   But° my outside to behold.

enclose   Gilded tombs do worms enfold.°

Had you been as wise as bold,   70

body   Young in limbs,° in judgment old,

Your answer had not been inscrolled.[2]

hopeless   Fare you well. Your suit is cold."°

Cold, indeed, and labor lost.

Then farewell heat, and welcome frost!   75

Portia, adieu. I have too grieved a heart

drawn-out   To take a tedious° leave. Thus losers part.

He exits [_with his train_].

Portia

A gentle riddance.—Draw the curtains; go.

—Let all of his complexion[3] choose me so.   _They exit._

1 *My daughter! O my ducats! O my daughter, / Fled with a Christian!*

Jay Halio (see For Further Reading) suggests that the fourteenth story in Masuccio's *Il novellino* is the likeliest source for the Jessica/Lorenzo subplot, although Marlowe's *The Jew of Malta*'s Barabas also has a daughter who betrays him. In Masuccio's tale, a miser's daughter falls in love with a young nobleman, who plots with a slave to trick the old man and elope with his daughter. She flees with her father's money, leaving him doubly bereft.

2 *Christian ducats*

Christian because they were earned in dealings with Christians and because they are now in Christian hands

3 *double ducats*

Gold coins each worth twice the single ducat

4 *stones*

Jewels (but with an unintended pun on *stones* meaning "testicles" picked up in the jeering reported in line 24)

Act 2, Scene 8

Enter **Salarino** *and* **Solanio**.

Salarino

Why, man, I saw Bassanio under sail.

With him is Gratiano gone along,

And in their ship I am sure Lorenzo is not.

Solanio

roused   The villain Jew with outcries raised° the Duke,

Who went with him to search Bassanio's ship.   5

Salarino

He came too late. The ship was under sail.

But there the Duke was given to understand

That in a gondola were seen together

Lorenzo and his amorous Jessica.

assured   Besides, Antonio certified° the Duke   10

They were not with Bassanio in his ship.

Solanio

outburst   I never heard a passion° so confused,

So strange, outrageous, and so variable

As the dog Jew did utter in the streets.

"My daughter! O my ducats! O my daughter,   15

Fled with a Christian!¹ O my Christian ducats!²

Justice, the law, my ducats, and my daughter!

A sealèd bag, two sealèd bags of ducats,

Of double ducats,³ stol'n from me by my daughter!

And jewels—two stones,⁴ two rich and precious

    stones—   20

Stol'n by my daughter! Justice! Find the girl!

She hath the stones upon her, and the ducats."

Salarino

Why, all the boys in Venice follow him,

Crying, "His stones, his daughter, and his ducats!"

1   *look he keep his day*

    **Be sure to meet the deadline (to
    repay the money he borrowed from
    Shylock).**

2   *the narrow seas*

    I.e., the English Channel

3   *fraught*

    Laden; filled with goods

4   *Slubber not business*

    Don't rush on your activities.

5   *stay the very riping of the time*

    **I.e., give yourself time for your
    plans fully to mature.**

6   *wondrous sensible*

    Deeply felt; very obvious

Solanio

Let good Antonio look he keep his day,[1]   25
Or he shall pay for this.

Salarino

                Marry, well remembered.

spoke   I reasoned° with a Frenchman yesterday,

Who told me, in the narrow seas[2] that part

was shipwrecked The French and English, there miscarrièd°

A vessel of our country richly fraught.[3]   30

about   I thought upon° Antonio when he told me

And wished in silence that it were not his.

Solanio

You were best to tell Antonio what you hear—

Yet do not suddenly, for it may grieve him.

Salarino

A kinder gentleman treads not the earth.   35

I saw Bassanio and Antonio part.

Bassanio told him he would make some speed

Of his return. He answered, "Do not so.

Slubber not business[4] for my sake, Bassanio,

But stay the very riping of the time,[5]   40

And for the Jew's bond which he hath of me,

thoughts   Let it not enter in your mind° of love.

Be merry and employ your chiefest thoughts

displays   To courtship and such fair ostents° of love

properly   As shall conveniently° become you there."   45

swollen   And even there, his eye being big° with tears,

Turning his face, he put his hand behind him,

And, with affection wondrous sensible,[6]

He wrung Bassanio's hand, and so they parted.

1   *he only loves the world for him*

    I.e., Antonio's pleasure in the world
    rests solely on his affection for
    Bassanio.

2   *quicken his embracèd heaviness*

    Liven up the sadness he has taken
    on; cheer him up

3   *Do we so.*

    Let us do it.

Solanio

I think he only loves the world for him.[1]   50

i.e., Antonio I pray thee, let us go and find him° out

And quicken his embracèd heaviness[2]

With some delight or other.

Salarino

                              Do we so.[3]   *They exit.*

1   *servitor*

    Servant

2   *Aragon*

    A region in northwest Spain

3   *to his election*

    To make his choice

4   *addressed me*

    Prepared myself

Act 2, Scene 9

Enter **Nerissa** *and a servitor.* [1]

Nerissa

Pull / right away Quick, quick, I pray thee. Draw° the curtain straight.°
The Prince of Aragon [2] hath ta'en his oath
And comes to his election [3] presently.

Enter [the Prince of] **Aragon**, *his train, and* **Portia**.

Portia

Behold; there stand the caskets, noble Prince.
the one If you choose that° wherein I am contained,   5
Straight shall our nuptial rites be solemnized.
But if you fail, without more speech, my lord,
You must be gone from hence immediately.

Aragon

bound I am enjoined° by oath to observe three things:
reveal First, never to unfold° to anyone   10
Which casket 'twas I chose; next, if I fail
Of the right casket, never in my life
To woo a maid in way of marriage;
Lastly, if I do fail in fortune of my choice,
Immediately to leave you and be gone.   15

Portia

To these injunctions everyone doth swear
unworthy That comes to hazard for my worthless° self.

Aragon

And so have I addressed me. [4] Fortune now
To my heart's hope! Gold, silver, and base lead.
"Who chooseth me must give and hazard all he hath."   20
i.e., The lead casket You° shall look fairer ere I give or hazard.

141

1   *be meant / By*

     Stand for

2   *but, like the martlet, / Builds in the*
     weather on the outward wall, / Even in
     the force and road of casualty

     But instead, like the house martin
     (a small swallow-like bird), builds
     its nest on the outer wall, even
     though that places it in the path of
     danger

3   *How many then should cover that stand*
     bare?

     How many people would be able
     to keep their hats on, rather than
     be forced to remove them (as a
     sign of deference to undeserving
     superiors)?

4   *new varnished*

     Restored to its former luster

5   *assume desert*

     Claim what I deserve

What says the golden chest? Ha, let me see.

"Who chooseth me shall gain what many men desire."

"What many men desire"—that "many" may be meant

By[1] the fool multitude that choose by show,   25

foolish   Not learning more than the fond° eye doth teach,

looks   Which pries° not to th' interior, but, like the martlet,

Builds in the weather on the outward wall,

Even in the force and road of casualty.[2]

I will not choose what many men desire   30

agree   Because I will not jump° with common spirits

myself   And rank me° with the barbarous multitudes.

Why, then, to thee, thou silver treasure house.

Tell me once more what title thou dost bear.

"Who chooseth me shall get as much as he deserves."   35

And well said too—for who shall go about

cheat   To cozen° fortune and be honorable

mark   Without the stamp° of merit? Let none presume

To wear an undeservèd dignity.

social ranks   Oh, that estates, degrees,° and offices   40

Were not derived corruptly, and that clear honor

Were purchased by the merit of the wearer!

How many then should cover that stand bare?[3]

would be / that now   How many be° commanded that° command?

separated   How much low peasantry would then be gleaned°   45

From the true seed of honor? And how much honor

Picked from the chaff and ruin of the times

To be new varnished?[4] Well, but to my choice.

"Who chooseth me shall get as much as he deserves."

I will assume desert.[5]—Give me a key for this   50

And instantly unlock my fortunes here.

> [*He is handed a key and opens the silver casket.*]

Portia

Too long a pause for that which you find there.

1   *To offend and judge are distinct offices*

    I.e., one cannot simultaneously be
    the defendant and the judge; you
    cannot be the judge in your own
    case.

2   *shadows*

    Images (portraits); illusions

3   *Silvered o'er*

    With silver decorations

4   *Take what wife you will to bed*

    The terms of the choosing, how-
    ever, prescribe that "if you choose
    wrong, / Never to speak to lady
    afterward / In way of marriage"
    (2.1.40–42; see also 2.9.11–13).

5   *Thus hath the candle singed the moth.*

    I.e., In just this way, the seeker has
    been burned by the thing he seeks.

Aragon

What's here? The portrait of a blinking idiot

scroll   Presenting me a schedule!° I will read it.

How much unlike art thou to Portia!   55

How much unlike my hopes and my deservings!

"Who chooseth me shall have as much as he deserves"?

Did I deserve no more than a fool's head?

due rewards   Is that my prize? Are my deserts° no better?

Portia

To offend and judge are distinct offices[1]   60

And of opposèd natures.

Aragon

                What is here?

purified / i.e., the silver   [*reads*] "The fire seven times tried° this,°

Seven times tried that judgment is,

wrongly   That did never choose amiss.°

Some there be that shadows[2] kiss.   65

Such have but a shadow's bliss.

certainly   There be fools alive, iwis,°

Silvered o'er[3]—and so was this.

want   Take what wife you will° to bed,[4]

i.e., The fool's portrait   I° will ever be your head.   70

done   So be gone. You are sped."°

—Still more fool I shall appear

By the time I linger here.

With one fool's head I came to woo,

But I go away with two.   75

—Sweet, adieu. I'll keep my oath

anger   Patiently to bear my wroth.°   [*He exits with his train.*]

Portia

Thus hath the candle singed the moth.[5]

deliberating   O these deliberate° fools! When they do choose,

They have the wisdom by their wit to lose.   80

1   *sensible regreets*

     Tangible greetings (i.e., gifts)

2   *commends and courteous breath*

     Compliments and courteous words

3   *high-day wit*

     Holiday (extravagant) language

4   *Bassanio, Lord Love, if thy will it be.*

     **(Let it be) Bassanio, Lord Cupid, if
     you are willing.**

Nerissa

The ancient saying is no heresy:

Hanging and wiving goes by destiny.

Portia

Come; draw the curtain, Nerissa.

Enter **Messenger**.

Messenger

Where is my lady?

Portia

                                    Here. What would my lord?

Messenger

arrived   Madam, there is alighted° at your gate   85

         A young Venetian, one that comes before

announce   To signify° th' approaching of his lord,

         From whom he bringeth sensible regrets, [1]

         To wit—besides commends and courteous breath [2]—

Before now   Gifts of rich value. Yet° I have not seen   90

         So likely an ambassador of love.

         A day in April never came so sweet

lush; bountiful   To show how costly° summer was at hand,

forerunner   As this forespurrer° comes before his lord.

Portia

         No more, I pray thee. I am half afeard   95

         Thou wilt say anon he is some kin to thee,

         Thou spend'st such high-day wit [3] in praising him.

         —Come, come, Nerissa, for I long to see

messenger   Quick Cupid's post° that comes so mannerly.

Nerissa

         Bassanio, Lord Love, if thy will it be. [4]   *They exit.*   100

1   *yet it lives there unchecked*

Now there is an uncontradicted
rumor circulating

2   *The Goodwins*

The Goodwin Sands, a shoal off
the southeastern coast of England,
where shipwrecks often occurred

3   *my gossip Report*

The rumor is here personified as
an idle-talking or information-
providing woman.

4   *I would she were as lying a gossip in*
that as ever knapped ginger or made her
neighbors believe she wept for the death
of a third husband.

I wish that she (the rumor) were
as untruthful as anyone who ever
munched ginger (an idiom for
"made up a spicy story"), or who
made her neighbors believe she
cried insincerely at her third husband's death.

5   *slips of prolixity*

I.e., long-winded lies

6   *crossing the plain highway of talk*

Diverging from the simple path of
truth

7   *oh, that I had a title good enough to keep*
his name company

Solanio wishes he had a more
appropriate epithet—rather than
honest or *good*—properly to convey
Antonio's virtues.

8   *Come, the full stop.*

Come to the period at the end of
your sentence; i.e., get to the point
of your talk.

Act 3, Scene 1

[*Enter*] **Solanio** *and* **Salarino**.

Solanio

Now, what news on the Rialto?

Salarino

Why, yet it lives there unchecked[1] that Antonio hath a
ship of rich lading° wracked° on the narrow seas. The
Goodwins[2] I think they call the place—a very dangerous
flat,° and fatal, where the carcasses of many a tall ship   5
lie buried, as they say, if my gossip Report[3] be an
honest woman of her word.

cargo / shipwrecked

sandbar

Solanio

I would she were as lying a gossip in that as ever
knapped ginger or made her neighbors believe she
wept for the death of a third husband.[4] But it is true,   10
without any slips of prolixity[5] or crossing the plain
highway of talk,[6] that the good Antonio, the honest
Antonio—oh, that I had a title good enough to keep
his name company![7]—

Salarino

Come, the full stop.[8]   15

Solanio

Ha, what sayest thou? Why, the end° is he hath lost a ship.

point

Salarino

I would it might prove the end of his losses.

Solanio

Let me say "amen" betimes,° lest the devil cross° my
prayer, for here he° comes in the likeness of a Jew.

quickly / thwart

i.e., the devil

Enter **Shylock**.

How now, Shylock? What news among the merchants?   20

1   *wings*

I.e., Jessica's page's costume (which permits her flight, and hence the metaphor that is also picked up in Solanio's speech following)

2   *fledged*

Feathered; ready to leave the nest (i.e., old enough to be married)

3   *flesh and blood*

Shylock is referring to Jessica, his child, but Solanio in line 31 derisively takes him to mean his sexual desire.

4   *Out upon it, old carrion!*

I.e., forget about it, you piece of rotting flesh!

5   *the mart*

I.e., the Exchange at the end of the Rialto (see 1.3.17 and note)

6   *look to his bond*

Remember his debt

7   *for a Christian court'sy*

Out of Christian generosity

Shylock

You knew—none so well, none so well as you—of my
daughter's flight.

Salarino

That's certain. I, for my part, knew the tailor that made
with the wings¹ she flew withal.°

Solanio

And Shylock, for his own part, knew the bird was   25
nature fledged,² and then it is the complexion° of them all to
mother (i.e., parent) leave the dam.°

Shylock

She is damned for it.

Salarino

That's certain, if the devil may be her judge.

Shylock

My own flesh and blood³ to rebel.   30

Solanio

Out upon it, old carrion.⁴ Rebels it at these years?

Shylock

mean I say° my daughter is my flesh and blood.

Salarino

There is more difference between thy flesh and hers
(a shiny black mineral) than between jet° and ivory, more between your
i.e., white wine bloods than there is between red wine and Rhenish.°   35
But tell us, do you hear whether Antonio have had any
loss at sea or no?

Shylock

bargain There I have another bad match.° A bankrupt, a prodigal
who dare scarce show his head on the Rialto, a beggar
accustomed that was used° to come so smug upon the mart.⁵ Let him   40
accustomed look to his bond.⁶ He was wont° to call me usurer. Let
him look to his bond. He was wont to lend money for a
Christian court'sy.⁷ Let him look to his bond.

1   *hindered me half a million*

    Kept me from making *half a million*
    ducats; or possibly, obstructed me
    half a million **times.**

2   *his humility*

    I.e., the Christian's compassion

3   *it shall go hard but I will better the*
    instruction

    Unless I'm very unlucky I will outdo
    what I have been taught.

4   *We have been up and down to seek him.*

    We have looked everywhere for
    him.

Salarino

Why, I am sure if he forfeit thou wilt not take his flesh.
What's that good for?   45

Shylock

To bait fish withal. If it will feed nothing else, it will
feed my revenge. He hath disgraced me and hindered
me half a million,[1] laughed at my losses, mocked at my
gains, scorned my nation, thwarted my bargains,

alienated / inflamed   cooled° my friends, heated° mine enemies. And what's   50
his reason? I am a Jew. Hath not a Jew eyes? Hath not
proportions   a Jew hands, organs, dimensions,° senses, affections,
passions? Fed with the same food, hurt with the same
weapons, subject to the same diseases, healed by the
same means, warmed and cooled by the same winter   55
and summer as a Christian is? If you prick us, do we not
bleed? If you tickle us, do we not laugh? If you poison
us, do we not die? And if you wrong us, shall we not
revenge? If we are like you in the rest, we will resemble
you in that. If a Jew wrong a Christian, what is his   60
humility?[2] Revenge. If a Christian wrong a Jew, what
i.e., response   should his sufferance° be by Christian example? Why,
revenge. The villainy you teach me I will execute—and
it shall go hard but I will better the instruction.[3]

Servingman   *Enter a **Man**° from Antonio.*

Man

[*to **Solanio** and **Salarino**] Gentlemen, my master Anto-   65
nio is at his house and desires to speak with you both.

Salarino

We have been up and down to seek him.[4]

        *Enter **Tubal**.*

1   *be matched*

Be found to equal them

2   *Frankfurt*

German city and the site of a well-
known jewelry market

3   *The curse*

Christian teaching (following Matthew 27:24–25) held that a curse
was placed upon the Jews for their
role in the crucifixion of Jesus.

4   *an argosy cast away*

A merchant ship lost

Solanio

i.e., tribe of Jews   Here comes another of the tribe.° A third cannot be
matched¹ unless the devil himself turn Jew.

[**Solanio**, **Salarino**, *and* **Man**] *exit.*

Shylock

How now, Tubal? What news from Genoa? Hast thou   70
found my daughter?

Tubal

I often came where I did hear of her, but cannot find her.

Shylock

Why, there, there, there, there! A diamond gone cost
me two thousand ducats in Frankfurt.² The curse³
never fell upon our nation till now. I never felt it till   75
now. Two thousand ducats in that, and other pre-
cious, precious jewels. I would my daughter were dead
i.e., I wish   at my foot, and the jewels in her ear. Would° she were
in a coffin   hearsed° at my foot, and the ducats in her coffin! No
news of them? Why, so; and I know not what's spent   80
in the search. Why thou, loss upon loss! The thief
gone with so much, and so much to find the thief, and
no satisfaction, no revenge. Nor no ill luck stirring but
upon / of   what lights o'° my shoulders, no sighs but o'° my
breathing, no tears but o' my shedding.   85

Tubal

Yes, other men have ill luck too. Antonio, as I heard in
Genoa—

Shylock

What, what, what? Ill luck, ill luck?

Tubal

Hath an argosy cast away⁴ coming from Tripoli.

Shylock

I thank God! I thank God! Is it true; is it true?   90

1   *Heard*

I.e., this is what you have heard

2   *break*

Go bankrupt

3   *Bespeak him a fortnight before.*

Hire him two weeks before
Antonio's loan is due.

4   *what merchandise I will*

Whatever deals I want

Tubal

shipwreck   I spoke with some of the sailors that escaped the wrack.°

Shylock

I thank thee, good Tubal. Good news, good news! Ha, ha! Heard¹ in Genoa?

Tubal

Your daughter spent in Genoa, as I heard, one night
eighty   fourscore° ducats.   95

Shylock

Thou stick'st a dagger in me. I shall never see my gold again. Fourscore ducats at a sitting? Fourscore ducats!

Tubal

several   There came divers° of Antonio's creditors in my company to Venice that swear he cannot choose but break.²

Shylock

I am very glad of it. I'll plague him; I'll torture him. I   100
am glad of it.

Tubal

from   One of them showed me a ring that he had of° your
in exchange for   daughter for° a monkey.

Shylock

Out upon her! Thou torturest me, Tubal. It was my turquoise. I had it of Leah when I was a bachelor.   105
I would not have given it for a wilderness of monkeys.

Tubal

But Antonio is certainly undone.

Shylock

hire   Nay, that's true; that's very true. Go, Tubal, fee° me an
sheriff's deputy   officer.° Bespeak him a fortnight before.³—I will have
i.e., Antonio   the heart of him° if he forfeit, for were he out of Venice   110
I can make what merchandise I will.⁴—Go, Tubal, and meet me at our synagogue. Go, good Tubal. At our synagogue, Tubal.   *They exit [separately].*

1   *in choosing*

If you choose

2   *Hate counsels not in such a quality*

I.e., if I hated you I would not speak
in this manner.

3   *hath no tongue but thought*

I.e., is not allowed openly to say
what she thinks

4   *am forsworn*

Have broken my oath

5   *So will I never be. So may you miss me*

An oath breaker I'll never be (i.e.,
I'll never tell you which chest to
choose). Therefore you might
choose incorrectly.

6   *But if you do you'll make me wish a sin, /*
     That I had been forsworn

·   But if you do (choose the wrong
casket), I'll wish that I had sinned by
breaking my oath to my father.

7   *Prove it so, / Let fortune go to Hell for it,*
     not I.

If it turns out (that we cannot be
together), blame fortune for it,
not me.

8   *as I am, I live upon the rack*

In my current state, I live as though
stretched upon *the rack* (a torture
device often used to compel con-
fessions from political prisoners).

Act 3, Scene 2

Enter **Bassanio**, **Portia**, *and all their trains,* [**Nerissa**, *and*]
Gratiano.

Portia

[*to* **Bassanio**] I pray you, tarry. Pause a day or two
Before you hazard, for in choosing¹ wrong

be patient   I lose your company. Therefore forbear° awhile.
There's something tells me (but it is not love)
I would not lose you, and you know yourself   5
Hate counsels not in such a quality.²
But lest you should not understand me well
(And yet a maiden hath no tongue but thought³)
I would detain you here some month or two
Before you venture for me. I could teach you   10
How to choose right, but then I am forsworn.⁴
So will I never be. So may you miss me,⁵
But if you do you'll make me wish a sin,

Curse   That I had been forsworn.⁶ Beshrew° your eyes;

bewitched   They have o'erlooked° me and divided me: 15
One half of me is yours, the other half yours—
Mine own, I would say—but if mine, then yours,

wicked   And so all yours. Oh, these naughty° times

barriers   Puts bars° between the owners and their rights.
And so, though yours, not yours. Prove it so,   20
Let fortune go to Hell for it, not I.⁷

slow down   I speak too long, but 'tis to peise° the time,

increase   To eke° it and to draw it out in length,

keep / choosing   To stay° you from election.°

Bassanio

                    Let me choose,
For as I am, I live upon the rack.⁸   25

1   *very sum*

Sum total

2   *swanlike end*

It was conventionally believed that
swans sang only once, while they
were dying.

3   *May stand more proper*

Might be more fitting; might apply
more precisely

Portia

Upon the rack, Bassanio? Then confess
What treason there is mingled with your love.

Bassanio

anxiety None but that ugly treason of mistrust,°
doubt Which makes me fear° th' enjoying of my love.
friendship There may as well be amity° and life   30
'Tween snow and fire, as treason and my love.

Portia

Ay, but I fear you speak upon the rack,
Where men enforcèd do speak anything.

Bassanio

Promise me life, and I'll confess the truth.

Portia

Well then, confess and live.

Bassanio

                              "Confess and love"   35
Had been the very sum¹ of my confession.
O happy torment, when my torturer
release Doth teach me answers for deliverance!°
But let me to my fortune and the caskets.

Portia

Away, then. I am locked in one of them.   40
If you do love me you will find me out.
aside —Nerissa and the rest, stand all aloof.°
Let music sound while he doth make his choice.
Then if he lose he makes a swanlike end,²
So that Fading in music. That° the comparison   45
i.e., tears May stand more proper,³ my eye° shall be the stream
And wat'ry deathbed for him. He may win,
And what is music then? Then music is
trumpet fanfare / loyal Even as the flourish° when true° subjects bow
To a new-crownèd monarch. Such it is   50

1   *creep into the dreaming bridegroom's*
    ear / And summon him to marriage
    **It was customary to play music
    under a bridegroom's window on
    the morning of his wedding.**

2   *Alcides, when he did redeem / The virgin*
    tribute paid by howling Troy / To the sea
    monster
    **Hercules (*Alcides*) kept the Trojan
    princess Hesione from being sac-
    rificed to a sea monster. He saved
    her not for love, but because he
    wanted her father's horses.**

3   *The rest aloof*
    **The others, standing aside (i.e.,
    Nerissa and the rest)**

4   *blearèd visages*
    Tear-stained faces

5   *Live thou*
    If you live

6   *mak'st the fray*
    Participate in the fight

7   *In the cradle*
    **I.e., in the eyes (the place from
    which love in its first, immature
    phase springs)**

8   *outward shows be least themselves*
    **Outward appearances be most
    deceiving**

melodious As are those dulcet° sounds in break of day

That creep into the dreaming bridegroom's ear

And summon him to marriage.¹ Now he goes

dignity With no less presence° but with much more love

Than young Alcides, when he did redeem   55

The virgin tribute paid by howling Troy

To the sea monster.² I stand for sacrifice.

Trojan The rest aloof³ are the Dardanian° wives,

With bleared visages⁴ come forth to view

outcome The issue° of th' exploit.—Go, Hercules!   60

Live thou,⁵ I live. With much, much more dismay

I view the fight than thou that mak'st the fray.⁶

A song the whilst **Bassanio** *comments on the caskets to himself.*

Singer

love   [*sings*] Tell me where is fancy° bred.

Either Or° in the heart or in the head?

How begot, how nourishèd?   65

All

Reply; reply.

Singer

conceived (*sings*) It is engendered° in the eyes,

With gazing fed, and fancy dies

In the cradle⁷ where it lies.

funeral bell Let us all ring fancy's knell.°   70

I'll begin it.—Ding, dong, bell.

All

Ding, dong, bell.

Bassanio

So may the outward shows be least themselves.⁸

always The world is still° deceived with ornament.

In law, what plea so tainted and corrupt   75

made appealing / pious But, being seasoned° with a gracious° voice,

Obscures the show of evil? In religion,

1   *some sober brow*

Some serious face (i.e., a clergyman)

2   *approve it with a text*

Validate it using a passage from
the Bible

3   *inward searched*

I.e., if their internal organs were
examined

4   *livers white as milk*

The liver was thought to be the seat
of human courage; a *white* or light-
colored liver indicated cowardice.

5   *And these assume but valor's excrement /
To render them redoubted*

And these cowards have nothing
more than the external marks of
valor (i.e., their *beards*) to make
themselves feared.

6   *purchased by the weight*

I.e., the result of cosmetics
(Makeup was sold by weight)

7   *lightest*

Most immoral (but punning on
"light" meaning "not heavy" following line 89)

8   *maketh such wanton gambols*

Dances so sensuously (i.e., with the
hair fluttering in the breeze)

9   *dowry of a second head*

I.e., a wig (made from the hair of a
dead person)

10 *Indian*

Indian (i.e., West Indian), and
therefore dark-skinned. (The Elizabethans conventionally associated
beauty with a fair complexion.)

11 *Midas*

A king of classical mythology,
simultaneously blessed and cursed
with the ability to turn all he
touched into gold, including his
food and, eventually, his daughter

12 *common drudge*

Servant at everyone's command
(probably referring to silver's
common use as a form of monetary
exchange)

13 *fleet to*

Dissolve into

14 *rash-embraced*

Too quickly accepted

What damnèd error, but some sober brow[1]

Will bless it and approve it with a text,[2]

Hiding the grossness with fair ornament? 80

absolute / it displays There is no vice so simple° but assumes°

its Some mark of virtue on his° outward parts.

How many cowards whose hearts are all as false

nonetheless As stairs of sand wear yet° upon their chins

Roman god of war The beards of Hercules and frowning Mars,° 85

Who, inward searched,[3] have livers white as milk,[4]

And these assume but valor's excrement

To render them redoubted.[5] Look on beauty,

And you shall see 'tis purchased by the weight,[6]

Which therein works a miracle in nature 90

Making them lightest[7] that wear most of it.

curly / hair So are those crispèd° snaky golden locks,°

Which maketh such wanton gambols[8] with the wind,

Upon supposèd fairness, often known

To be the dowry of a second head,[9] 95

i.e., the hairs / grave The skull that bred them° in the sepulcher.°

treacherous; deceptive Thus ornament is but the guilèd° shore

To a most dangerous sea, the beauteous scarf

Veiling an Indian[10] beauty—in a word,

The seeming truth which cunning times put on 100

To entrap the wisest. Therefore, then, thou gaudy gold,

Hard food for Midas,[11] I will none of thee.

Nor none of thee, thou pale and common drudge[12]

poor 'Tween man and man. But thou, thou meager° lead,

anything Which rather threaten'st than dost promise aught,° 105

Thy paleness moves me more than eloquence,

And here choose I. Joy be the consequence!

Portia

[*aside*] How all the other passions fleet to[13] air,

Such as As° doubtful thoughts, and rash-embracèd[14] despair,

1   *What demigod / Hath come so near*
    creation?

    **What godlike artist has painted this
    lifelike portrait?**

2   *Move these eyes?*

    **Do these eyes (i.e., the eyes in the
    portrait of Portia) move?**

3   *riding on the balls of mine*

    **I.e., reflected in my eyes (*balls* =
    eyeballs)**

4   *unfurnished*

    **Unaccompanied. (The painter,
    having been blinded by the beauty
    of Portia's first eye, will be unable
    to paint the second one.)**

5   *Yet look how far / The substance of my*
    praise doth wrong this shadow / In
    underprizing it, so far this shadow / Doth
    limp behind the substance.

    **But just as far as my praise for this
    picture underrates its beauty, the
    portrait itself is that much less
    beautiful than the living Portia.**

6   *Chance as fair*

    Have as much luck

7   *hold your fortune for your bliss*

    Consider this outcome a happy one.

8   *by note*

    I.e., as the scroll instructs

And shudd'ring fear, and green-eyed jealousy!   110

Calm   O love, be moderate. Allay° thy ecstasy.

moderation / Reduce   In measure° rein thy joy. Scant° this excess.

I feel too much thy blessing. Make it less,

For fear I surfeit.

Bassanio

[*opening the lead casket*] What find I here?

image   Fair Portia's counterfeit!° What demigod   115

Hath come so near creation?[1] Move these eyes?[2]

Or whether, riding on the balls of mine,[3]

opened   Seem they in motion? Here are severed° lips,

barrier   Parted with sugar breath. So sweet a bar°

i.e., Portia's lips   Should sunder such sweet friends.° Here in her hairs,   120

The painter plays the spider and hath woven

A golden mesh t' entrap the hearts of men

More firmly   Faster° than gnats in cobwebs. But her eyes—

How could he see to do them? Having made one,

Methinks it should have power to steal both his   125

And leave itself unfurnished.[4] Yet look how far

likeness   The substance of my praise doth wrong this shadow°

In underprizing it, so far this shadow

Doth limp behind the substance.[5] Here's the scroll,

container   The continent° and summary of my fortune: 130

[*reads*] "You that choose not by the view

Chance as fair[6] and choose as true.

Since this fortune falls to you,

Be content and seek no new.

If you be well pleased with this   135

And hold your fortune for your bliss,[7]

Turn you where your lady is

And claim her with a loving kiss."

A gentle scroll.—Fair lady, by your leave,

I come by note[8] to give and to receive.   140

1   *universal shout*

Shouts everywhere

2   *to term in gross*

To describe generally

3   *As from her lord, her governor, her king*

See Ephesians 5:22: "Wives submit your selves unto your husbands, as unto the Lord." While numerous domestic conduct books asserted this as a central tenet of marriage, the fact that they had to keep asserting it suggests that in real life marital relationships usually were much more complex.

<dl>
<dt>contest</dt>
</dl>

Like one of two contending in a prize°
That thinks he hath done well in people's eyes,
Hearing applause and universal shout,[1]
Giddy in spirit, still gazing in a doubt

for him Whether these peals of praise be his° or no, 145
So, thrice fair lady, stand I even so,
As doubtful whether what I see be true
Until confirmed, signed, ratified by you.

Portia

You see me, Lord Bassanio, where I stand
Such as I am. Though for myself alone 150
I would not be ambitious in my wish
To wish myself much better, yet for you
I would be trebled twenty times myself,
A thousand times more fair, ten thousand times more
    rich,

estimation That only to stand high in your account° 155
property I might in virtues, beauties, livings,° friends
computation Exceed account.° But the full sum of me
Is sum of something which, to term in gross,[2]
untutored/inexperienced Is an unlessoned° girl, unschooled, unpracticed;°
Fortunate Happy° in this: she is not yet so old 160
i.e., may still But she may° learn. Happier than this:
raised to be She is not bred° so dull but she can learn.
Happiest of all is that her gentle spirit
Commits itself to yours to be directed
As from her lord, her governor, her king.[3] 165
Myself and what is mine to you and yours
Just Is now converted. But° now I was the lord
Of this fair mansion, master of my servants,
queen o'er myself. And even now, but now,
This house, these servants, and this same myself 170
Are yours, my lord's. I give them with this ring,

1   *And be my vantage to exclaim on you*

     And provide me the opportunity to denounce you

2   *Where every something, being blent together, / Turns to a wild of nothing, save of joy*

     Where everything that is said, jumbled together, turns into an unintelligible din that expresses only the general sense of delight

3   *can wish none from me*

     I.e., do not need any added joy from me (or, cannot in any way lessen my own happiness)

4   *solemnize / The bargain of your faith*

     I.e., marry

5   *maid*

     Nerissa is not a domestic servant but a waiting gentlewoman, or companion, like Maria in *Twelfth Night*.

Which when you part from, lose, or give away,

foreshadow Let it presage° the ruin of your love

And be my vantage to exclaim on you.[1]

[*gives* **Bassanio** *a ring*]

Bassanio

deprived Madam, you have bereft° me of all words.   175

Only my blood speaks to you in my veins,

mental faculties And there is such confusion in my powers°

As, after some oration fairly spoke

By a belovèd prince, there doth appear

Among the buzzing pleasèd multitude,   180

blended Where every something, being blent° together,

Turns to a wild of nothing, save of joy,[2]

Expressed and not expressed. But when this ring

i.e., my body Parts from this finger, then parts life from hence.°

Oh, then be bold to say Bassanio's dead!   185

Nerissa

My lord and lady, it is now our time,

Those who That° have stood by and seen our wishes prosper,

To cry, "Good joy, good joy, my lord and lady!"

Gratiano

My Lord Bassanio and my gentle lady,

I wish you all the joy that you can wish,   190

For I am sure you can wish none from me.[3]

And when your honors mean to solemnize

The bargain of your faith,[4] I do beseech you

Even at that time I may be married too.

Bassanio

provided that With all my heart, so° thou canst get a wife.   195

Gratiano

I thank your Lordship; you have got me one.

My eyes, my lord, can look as swift as yours.

You saw the mistress; I beheld the maid.[5]

1   *until I sweat again*

    **Until I did sweat again (i.e.,
    repeatedly)**

2   *provided that your fortune / Achieved her
    mistress*

    **As long as you were able to win
    Portia's hand**

3   *so you stand pleased withal*

    As long as you are happy with it

4   *mean good faith*

    **Mean this sincerely (with a glance at
    his future marital faithfulness)**

5   *We'll play with them the first boy for a
    thousand ducats.*

    **We'll bet them a thousand ducats
    that we have the first son.**

6   *stake down*

    **Take the bet (but Gratiano plays
    on the meaning "without an
    erection").**

delay   You loved; I loved, for intermission°

No more pertains to me, my lord, than you.   200

depended   Your fortune stood° upon the caskets there,

And so did mine too, as the matter falls.

For wooing here until I sweat again,[1]

i.e., roof of my mouth   And swearing till my very roof° was dry

With oaths of love, at last—if promise last—   205

from   I got a promise of° this fair one here

To have her love, provided that your fortune

Achieved her mistress.[2]

Portia

Is this true, Nerissa?

Nerissa

Madam, it is, so you stand pleased withal.[3]

Bassanio

And do you, Gratiano, mean good faith?[4]   210

Gratiano

i.e., in faith   Yes, faith,° my lord.

Bassanio

Our feast shall be much honored in your marriage.

Gratiano

[*to* **Nerissa**] We'll play with them the first boy for a

thousand ducats.[5]

Nerissa

What, and stake down?[6]   215

Gratiano

if   No, we shall ne'er win at that sport an° stake down.

Enter **Lorenzo, Jessica, Salerio,** *a messenger
from Venice.*

But who comes here? Lorenzo and his infidel? What,
and my old Venetian friend Salerio?

1   *If that the youth of my new interest here /*

    Have power to bid you welcome

  If the short time that I have been in this position (as master of the house) gives me the authority to welcome you

2   *past all saying nay*

  Beyond any ability to say no

3   *Commends him*

  Sends his greetings

Bassanio

Lorenzo and Salerio, welcome hither,

If that the youth of my new interest here   220

Have power to bid you welcome. [*to* **Portia**] By your
    leave,

true   I bid my very° friends and countrymen,

Sweet Portia, welcome.

Portia

                So do I, my lord.

They are entirely welcome.

Lorenzo

I thank your Honor. For my part, my lord,   225

My purpose was not to have seen you here,

But meeting with Salerio by the way,

He did entreat me, past all saying nay, [2]

To come with him along.

Salerio

              I did, my lord.

And I have reason for it. Signior Antonio   230

Commends him [3] to you.   [*gives* **Bassanio** *a letter*]

Bassanio

              Ere I ope his letter,

I pray you tell me how my good friend doth.

Salerio

Not sick, my lord, unless it be in mind,

Nor well, unless in mind. His letter there

condition   Will show you his estate.°   235

                   [**Bassanio**] *open*[*s*] *the letter.*

Gratiano

yonder   [*indicating* **Jessica**] Nerissa, cheer yond° stranger. Bid
    her welcome.

—Your hand, Salerio. What's the news from Venice?

How doth that royal merchant, good Antonio?

1   *We are the Jasons; we have won the fleece.*

Gratiano continues the comparison
between Bassanio and his men
and the mythical Jason and the
Argonauts (originally made in
1.1.170–172). Bassanio has been
successful in winning "the golden
fleece," or Portia. In addition to
alluding to Jason's pursuit of the
Golden Fleece, "fleece" also meant
booty or plunder.

2   *fleece*

Salerio puns on the similarity of
sound between *fleece* and *fleets*.

3   *all the wealth I had / Ran in my veins*

Bassanio has no money, only aristocratic blood.

4   *feed my means*

Pay my expenses

5   *as*

Is like (i.e., ripped open)

pleased to hear	I know he will be glad° of our success.
	We are the Jasons; we have won the fleece.¹ 240
	Salerio
	I would you had won the fleece² that he hath lost.
	Portia
distressing	There are some shrewd° contents in yond same paper
	That steals the color from Bassanio's cheek.
otherwise	Some dear friend dead, else° nothing in the world
change / appearance	Could turn° so much the constitution° 245
confident; unflappable	Of any constant° man. What, worse and worse?
permission	—With leave,° Bassanio, I am half yourself,
	And I must freely have the half of anything
	That this same paper brings you.
	Bassanio
	O sweet Portia,
	Here are a few of the unpleasant'st words 250
stained	That ever blotted° paper. Gentle lady,
	When I did first impart my love to you,
	I freely told you all the wealth I had
	Ran in my veins.³ I was a gentleman,
	And then I told you true. And yet, dear lady, 255
Judging / to be worth	Rating° myself at° nothing, you shall see
	How much I was a braggart. When I told you
financial condition	My state° was nothing, I should then have told you
	That I was worse than nothing, for indeed
bound; contracted	I have engaged° myself to a dear friend, 260
absolute; deadly	Engaged my friend to his mere° enemy
	To feed my means.⁴ Here is a letter, lady,
	The paper as⁵ the body of my friend,
	And every word in it a gaping wound,
	Issuing life blood.—But is it true, Salerio? 265
success	Have all his ventures failed? What, not one hit?°
	From Tripoli, from Mexico and England,

1   *impeach the freedom of the state*

     **I.e., call into question the fairness
     of the government**

2   *go hard with*

     Be bad for

3   *any that draws breath*

     I.e., any person living

From Lisbon, Barbary, and India?
And not one vessel 'scape the dreadful touch
Of merchant-marring rocks?

Salerio

        Not one, my lord. 270
Besides, it should appear that if he had

available / repay The present° money to discharge° the Jew,
i.e., Shylock He° would not take it. Never did I know
A creature that did bear the shape of man
eager / destroy So keen° and greedy to confound° a man. 275
petitions He plies° the Duke at morning and at night
And doth impeach the freedom of the state[1]
If they deny him justice. Twenty merchants,
Venetian noblemen The Duke himself, and the magnificoes°
rank / argued Of greatest port° have all persuaded° with him, 280
malicious But none can drive him from the envious° plea
Of forfeiture, of justice, and his bond.

Jessica

When I was with him I have heard him swear
To Tubal and to Chus, his countrymen,
That he would rather have Antonio's flesh 285
Than twenty times the value of the sum
That he did owe him. And I know, my lord,
If law, authority, and power deny not,
It will go hard with[2] poor Antonio.

Portia

Is it your dear friend that is thus in trouble? 290

Bassanio

The dearest friend to me, the kindest man,
natured The best conditioned° and unwearied spirit
good deeds In doing courtesies,° and one in whom
The ancient Roman honor more appears
Than any that draws breath[3] in Italy. 295

1   *use your pleasure*

Do what you want.

Portia

What sum owes he the Jew?

Bassanio

For me, three thousand ducats.

Portia

What, no more?

cancel Pay him six thousand and deface° the bond!

Double six thousand, and then treble that,

Before a friend of this description 300

Shall lose a hair through Bassanio's fault.

First go with me to church and call me wife,

And then away to Venice to your friend,

For never shall you lie by Portia's side

With an unquiet soul. You shall have gold 305

trivial To pay the petty° debt twenty times over.

When it is paid, bring your true friend along.

My maid Nerissa and myself meantime

Will live as maids and widows. Come away,

leave For you shall hence° upon your wedding day. 310

disposition Bid your friends welcome; show a merry cheer.°

expensively / dearly Since you are dear° bought, I will love you dear.°

But let me hear the letter of your friend.

Bassanio

[*reads*] "Sweet Bassanio, my ships have all miscarried.

My creditors grow cruel. My estate is very low. My 315

bond to the Jew is forfeit, and, since in paying it, it is

impossible I should live, all debts are cleared between

merely you and I if I might but° see you at my death. Not-

withstanding, use your pleasure. ' If your love do not

persuade you to come, let not my letter." 320

1   *till I come again, / No bed shall e'er be*
guilty of my stay, / No rest be interposer
'twixt us twain

I.e., I won't sleep until I return to
you.

Portia

finish up   O love, dispatch° all business and be gone!

Bassanio

Since I have your good leave to go away,

I will make haste, but till I come again,

No bed shall e'er be guilty of my stay,

Nor rest be interposer 'twixt us twain. '   *They exit.*   325

1 *come abroad*

   Appear in public

2 *kept with*

   Lived among

Act 3, Scene 3

*Enter [**Shylock**] the Jew, and [**Solanio**] and **Antonio**, and the jailer.*

Shylock
Jailer, look to him. Tell not me of mercy.
i.e., without interest This is the fool that lent out money gratis.°
Jailer, look to him.

Antonio
                                    Hear me yet, good Shylock.

Shylock
I'll have my bond. Speak not against my bond.
I have sworn an oath that I will have my bond.   5
Thou called'st me dog before thou hadst a cause,
But since I am a dog beware my fangs.
The Duke shall grant me justice.—I do wonder,
wicked / foolish Thou naughty° jailer, that thou art so fond°
i.e., Antonio's To come abroad¹ with him at his° request.   10

Antonio
I pray thee, hear me speak.

Shylock
I'll have my bond. I will not hear thee speak.
I'll have my bond, and therefore speak no more.
stupid; gullible I'll not be made a soft and dull-eyed° fool
To shake the head, relent and sigh, and yield   15
To Christian intercessors. Follow not.
I'll have no speaking. I will have my bond.   *[He] exits.*

Solanio
It is the most impenetrable cur
That ever kept with² men.

Antonio
                                    Let him alone.
useless I'll follow him no more with bootless° prayers.   20

1   *I oft delivered from his forfeitures / Many*
     that have at times made moan to me
     **I have kept many people, who have
at various times come to me in
trouble, from defaulting on their
debts owed to Shylock.**

2   *Will much impeach the justice of the*
     state, / Since that the trade and profit of
     the city / Consisteth of all nations
     **Will significantly discredit Venice's
reputation for justice, which is
what allows *all nations* to trade
confidently with the city**

He seeks my life. His reason well I know.
I oft delivered from his forfeitures
Many that have at times made moan to me;[1]
Therefore he hates me.

Solanio

                 I am sure the Duke
Will never grant this forfeiture to hold.   25

Antonio

The Duke cannot deny the course of law.
For the commodity° that strangers have   *commercial privileges*
With us in Venice, if it be denied,
Will much impeach the justice of the state,
Since that the trade and profit of the city   30
Consisteth of all nations.[2] Therefore go.
These griefs and losses have so bated° me   *diminished*
That I shall hardly spare a pound of flesh
Tomorrow to my bloody creditor.
—Well, jailer, on. Pray God Bassanio come   35
To see me pay his debt, and then I care not.   *They exit.*

1   *appears most strongly / In bearing thus*
     the absence of your lord

     **Is most apparent now, as you deal
     with the absence of your husband**

2   *Than customary bounty can enforce you*

     **Than of what your usual kindness
     makes you do**

3   *for in companions*

     **See Sir Thomas Elyot's discussion
     of friendship in *The Book Named the
     Governor* (1531; reprinted, London
     1580): "it is a blessed and stable
     connection of sundry wills, making
     of two persons one in having and
     suffering. And therefore a friend
     is properly named of philosophers
     'the other I.' For that in them is but
     one mind and one possession; and
     that which more is, a man more re-
     joiceth in his friend's good fortune
     than at his own" (excerpted in Leah
     Marcus, ed., p. 107. See For Futher
     Reading).**

4   *the semblance of my soul*

     **The image of my soul (i.e., Antonio).
     Since Antonio is just like Bassanio
     and since Bassanio's soul is just like
     Portia's, Antonio's soul is then the
     image of Portia's.**

5   *comes too near*

     Sounds too much like

Act 3, Scene 4

Enter **Portia, Nerissa, Lorenzo, Jessica,** *and* [**Balthazar,**]
a man° of **Portia***'s.*

servant

Lorenzo

Madam, although I speak it in your presence,

You have a noble and a true conceit°   *understanding*

Of godlike amity, which appears most strongly

In bearing thus the absence of your lord. [1]

But if you knew to whom you show this honor,   5

How true a gentleman you send relief,

How dear a lover of my lord your husband,

I know you would be prouder of the work

Than customary bounty can enforce you. [2]

Portia

I never did repent for doing good,   10

Nor shall not now; for in companions [3]

That do converse and waste° the time together,   *spend*

Whose souls do bear an equal yoke° of love,   *connection; tie*

There must be needs° a like° proportion   *necessarily / similar*

Of lineaments,° of manners, and of spirit,   *characteristics*   15

Which makes me think that this Antonio,

Being the bosom lover of my lord,

Must needs be like my lord. If it be so,

How little is the cost I have bestowed°   *spent*

In purchasing the semblance of my soul [4]   20

From out° the state of hellish cruelty!   *out of*

This comes too near [5] the praising of myself.

Therefore no more of it. Hear other things:

Lorenzo, I commit into your hands

The husbandry° and manage° of my house   *care / management*   25

Until my lord's return. For mine own part,

I have toward Heaven breathed° a secret vow   *whispered*

189

1   *all th' endeavor of man*

Everything humanly possible

2   *Padua*

Both Q and F read "Mantua," but
4.1.109 and 5.1.268 make it clear
that Padua, which was the chief
center of Italian legal studies, is
intended.

To live in prayer and contemplation,
Only attended by Nerissa here,
Until her husband and my lord's return.   30
There is a monastery two miles off,
And there will we abide. I do desire you
command Not to deny this imposition,°
The which my love and some necessity
Now lays upon you.

Lorenzo

                 Madam, with all my heart,   35
I shall obey you in all fair commands.

Portia

servants My people° do already know my mind
And will acknowledge you and Jessica
In place of Lord Bassanio and myself.
So fare you well till we shall meet again.   40

Lorenzo

Fair thoughts and happy hours attend on you!

Jessica

I wish your Ladyship all heart's content.

Portia

I thank you for your wish and am well pleased
To wish it back on you. Fare you well, Jessica.

                   [**Jessica** *and* **Lorenzo**] *exit.*

Now, Balthazar,   45
As I have ever found thee honest true,
So let me find thee still. Take this same letter
And use thou all th' endeavor of a man[1]
hurrying / deliver In speed° to Padua.[2] See thou render° this

                   [*hands him a paper*]

Into my cousin's hands, Doctor Bellario,   50
whatever And look what° notes and garments he doth give thee.
all conceivable Bring them, I pray thee, with imagined° speed

1   *that we lack*

     That which we do not have (i.e.,
     penises)

2   *between the change of man and boy*

     I.e., as though I were an adolescent
     (whose voice cracks)

3   *I could not do withal!*

     I could not do anything about it!

4   *Above a twelvemonth*

     Over a year ago

ferry / public   Unto the traject,° to the common° ferry
goes back and forth   Which trades° to Venice. Waste no time in words,

But get thee gone. I shall be there before thee.   55

Balthazar

appropriate   Madam, I go with all convenient° speed.   [*He exits.*]

Portia

Come on, Nerissa; I have work in hand

That you yet know not of. We'll see our husbands

Before they think of us.

Nerissa

                Shall they see us?

Portia

costume   They shall, Nerissa, but in such a habit°   60

equipped   That they shall think we are accomplishèd°

With that we lack.¹ I'll hold thee any wager,

dressed   When we are both accoutred° like young men,

I'll prove the prettier fellow of the two,

And wear my dagger with the braver grace,   65

And speak between the change of man and boy²

squeaking   With a reed° voice, and turn two mincing steps

fights   Into a manly stride, and speak of frays°

elaborate   Like a fine bragging youth, and tell quaint° lies

How honorable ladies sought my love,   70

Which I denying, they fell sick and died—

I could not do withal!³—then I'll repent

in spite of   And wish, for° all that, that I had not killed them.

And twenty of these puny lies I'll tell,

That men shall swear I have discontinued school   75

Above a twelvemonth.⁴ I have within my mind

immature / knaves   A thousand raw° tricks of these bragging jacks°

Which I will practice.

1   *turn to*

    Be transformed into. (Portia's
    reply recognizes the potential
    meaning "seek out men for sexual
    pleasure.")

2   *if thou wert near a lewd interpreter*

    If you were near someone with a
    dirty mind

Nerissa

        Why, shall we turn to ' men?

Portia

Fie, what a question's that,

If thou wert near a lewd interpreter![2]   80

plan   But come; I'll tell thee all my whole device°

waits   When I am in my coach, which stays° for us

    At the park gate. And therefore haste away,

travel   For we must measure° twenty miles today.   *They exit.*

1   *agitation*

I.e., cogitation (understanding)

2   *bastard hope*

Unlikely possibility (with a pun on the literal sense: the hope you are a bastard, i.e., not Shylock's child; see lines 11–12)

3   *the sins of my mother*

I.e., the sin of giving birth out of wedlock

4   *when I shun Scylla your father, I fall into Charybdis your mother*

I.e., I am caught in an impossible situation. In Homer's *Odyssey*, *Scylla* was a monster who lived under the rocks that lay on one side of the Straits of Messina. On the other side of the straits was the whirlpool *Charybdis*, making passage through the channel extremely difficult, with dangers on either side.

5   *gone*

Doomed (i.e., *gone* to Hell)

6   *one by another*

I.e., as neighbors

7   *If we grow all to be pork-eaters, we shall not shortly have a rasher on the coals for money.*

I.e, if all the Jews convert to Christianity, there will be more people eating pork (since Jews are forbidden to do so) and the increased demand will make it impossible to find a grilled piece of bacon at any price.

Act 3, Scene 5

*Enter [**Launcelot** the] clown and **Jessica**.*

Launcelot

Yes, truly, for look you, the sins of the father are to be
laid upon the children. Therefore I promise you I fear°
you. I was always plain with you, and so now I speak my
agitation[1] of the matter. Therefore be o' good cheer,
for truly I think you are damned. There is but one   5
hope in it that can do you any good, and that is but a
kind of bastard hope[2] neither.°

fear for (gloss for line 2)

i.e., in any case (gloss for line 7)

Jessica

And what hope is that, I pray thee?

Launcelot

Marry, you may partly hope that your father got° you
not, that you are not the Jew's daughter.   10

begot; sired (gloss for line 9)

Jessica

That were a kind of bastard hope indeed. So the sins
of my mother[3] should be visited upon me.

Launcelot

Truly then, I fear you are damned both by father and
mother. Thus when I shun Scylla your father, I fall into
Charybdis your mother.[4] Well, you are gone[5] both ways.   15

Jessica

I shall be saved by my husband. He hath made me a
Christian.

Launcelot

Truly, the more to blame he. We were Christians
enough before, e'en as many as could well live one by
another.[6] This making of Christians will raise the price   20
of hogs. If we grow all to be pork-eaters, we shall not
shortly have a rasher on the coals for money.[7]

1   *getting up of the negro's belly*

Getting the *negro* (the *Moor*)
pregnant

2   *more than reason*

I.e., bigger than she should be (with
a pun on *Moor* and *more*)

3   *if she be less than an honest woman, she*
    is indeed more than I took her for

I.e., if she is unchaste, that is still
better than I thought she would be.

4   *play upon the word*

Engage in wordplay

5   *best grace*

Most attractive feature

6   *grow commendable*

Be praiseworthy

Enter **Lorenzo**.

Jessica

I'll tell my husband, Launcelot, what you say. Here he
comes.

Lorenzo

I shall grow jealous of you shortly, Launcelot, if you   25
thus get my wife into corners.

Jessica

Nay, you need not fear us, Lorenzo. Launcelot and I are
arguing; at odds   out.° He tells me flatly there is no mercy for me in
Heaven because I am a Jew's daughter, and he says
you are no good member of the commonwealth, for   30
in converting Jews to Christians you raise the price of
pork.

Lorenzo

explain   I shall answer° that better to the commonwealth than
you can the getting up of the negro's belly.[1] The Moor
is with child by you, Launcelot.   35

Launcelot

a serious matter   It is much° that the Moor should be more than reason,[2]
chaste   but if she be less than an honest° woman, she is
indeed more than I took her for.[3]

Lorenzo

How every fool can play upon the word![4] I think the
best grace[5] of wit will shortly turn into silence, and   40
discourse grow commendable[6] in none only but par-
rots. Go in, sirrah. Bid them prepare for dinner.

Launcelot

appetites   That is done, sir. They have all stomachs.°

Lorenzo

punster   Goodly Lord, what a wit-snapper° are you! Then bid
them prepare dinner.   45

1   *cover*

     Set the table (but in line 48 Launce-
     lot plays on the meaning "cover
     one's head with a hat")

2   *my duty*

     I.e., to remain bareheaded before
     social superiors

3   *quarreling with occasion*

     Quibbling at every opportunity

4   *humors and conceits*

     Whims and fancies

5   *suited*

     Made to fit; adapted to the matter
     at hand (referring to Launcelot's
     gift for clever wordplay), but per-
     haps also with the sense of "part of
     his fool's outfit"

6   *A many fools that stand in better place*

     Many fools with more elevated
     positions

7   *tricksy*

     Ambiguous (i.e., a word that is
     easily adapted to wordplay)

8   *Defy the matter*

     Fail to speak plainly; confuse the
     meaning

9   *How cheer'st thou*

     How do you feel?

10   *if on Earth he do not merit it, / In reason*
     he should never come to Heaven

     If on Earth he does not deserve it
     (i.e., the blessing that is Portia)
     by living uprightly, it follows that
     he should never be allowed into
     Heaven.

Launcelot

That is done too, sir. Only "cover!" [1] is the word.

Lorenzo

Will you cover then, sir?

Launcelot

Not so, sir, neither. I know my duty. [2]

Lorenzo

Yet more quarreling with occasion! [3] Wilt thou show
the whole wealth of thy wit in an instant? I pray thee,   50
understand a plain man in his plain meaning. Go to thy
food   fellows, bid them cover the table, serve in the meat, °
and we will come in to dinner.

Launcelot

For the table, sir, it shall be served in. For the meat, sir,
it shall be covered. For your coming in to dinner, sir,   55
why, let it be as humors and conceits [4] shall govern.

Clown exits.

Lorenzo

O dear discretion, how his words are suited! [5]
The fool hath planted in his memory
An army of good words, and I do know
A many fools that stand in better place, [6]   60
Furnished (with words) Garnished ° like him, that for a tricksy [7] word
Defy the matter. [8] How cheer'st thou, [9] Jessica?
And now, good sweet, say thy opinion.
How dost thou like the Lord Bassanio's wife?

Jessica

fitting   Past all expressing. It is very meet °   65
honorable   The Lord Bassanio live an upright ° life,
For having such a blessing in his lady,
He finds the joys of Heaven here on Earth.
And if on Earth he do not merit it,
In reason he should never come to Heaven. [10]   70

1   *there must be something else / Pawned*
     with the other

     Something more must be bet
     along with the other woman.
     (Since no woman is equal to
     Portia, the bet would not be
     equal otherwise.)

2   *set you forth*

     (1) serve you dinner; (2) sing your
     praises

contest Why, if two gods should play some heavenly match°
And on the wager lay two earthly women,
is one (of the two) And Portia one,° there must be something else
unrefined Pawned with the other,¹ for the poor rude° world
equal Hath not her fellow.°

Lorenzo

        Even such a husband   75
Hast thou of me as she is for a wife.

Jessica

Nay, but ask my opinion too of that!

Lorenzo

soon I will anon.° First let us go to dinner.

Jessica

appetite Nay, let me praise you while I have a stomach.°

Lorenzo

No, pray thee, let it serve for table talk.   80
however Then howsome'er° thou speak'st, 'mong other things
I shall digest it.

Jessica

        Well, I'll set you forth.²   [They] exit.

1   *armed*

Mentally prepared

Act 4, Scene 1

Enter the **Duke**, *the magnificoes*,° **Antonio**, **Bassanio**,
Gratiano, [**Salerio**, *and attendants*].

Duke

What, is Antonio here?

Antonio

Ready, so please your Grace.

Duke

defend yourself against I am sorry for thee. Thou art come to answer°

A stony adversary, an inhuman wretch

Uncapable of pity, void and empty   5

tiny amount From any dram° of mercy.

Antonio

                 I have heard

moderate Your Grace hath ta'en great pains to qualify°

unyielding His rigorous course. But since he stands obdurate,°

And that no lawful means can carry me

malice's Out of his envy's° reach, I do oppose   10

against My patience to° his fury and am armed¹

To suffer with a quietness of spirit

cruelty The very tyranny° and rage of his.

Duke

Go, one, and call the Jew into the court.

Salerio

He is ready at the door. He comes, my lord.   15

Enter **Shylock**.

Duke

i.e., my (the royal plural) Make room and let him stand before our° face.

    —Shylock, the world thinks, and I think so too,

1   *thou but leadest this fashion of thy malice /*
    To the last hour of act

    **I.e., you are only pretending to
    insist on your pound of flesh until
    the last possible moment.**

2   *more strange*

    **More extraordinary (though *strange*
    in line 21 means "abnormal" or
    even "alien")**

3   *Glancing an eye of pity*

    Looking with pity

4   *of late*

    Recently

5   *commiseration of his state*

    Pity for his condition

6   *offices of tender courtesy*

    Acts of gentle kindness

7   *gentle*

    Kind (with a pun on "gentile")

8   *gaping pig*

    A pig roasted with its mouth open

9   *sings i' th' nose*

    Makes its nasal sound

That thou but leadest this fashion of thy malice

To the last hour of act,[1] and then 'tis thought

Thou wilt / pity Thou'lt° show thy mercy and remorse° more strange[2]   20

Than is thy strange apparent cruelty;

And where thou now exacts the penalty,

Which is a pound of this poor merchant's flesh,

release Thou wilt not only loose° the forfeiture

But, touched with human gentleness and love,   25

portion Forgive a moiety° of the principal,

Glancing an eye of pity[3] on his losses

piled That have of late[4] so huddled° on his back,

Enough to press a royal merchant down

And pluck commiseration of his state[5]   30

pitiless From brassy° bosoms and rough hearts of flint,

From stubborn Turks and Tartars never trained

To offices of tender courtesy.[6]

We all expect a gentle[7] answer, Jew.

Shylock

informed / intend I have possessed° your Grace of what I purpose,°   35

And by our holy Sabbath have I sworn

To have the due and forfeit of my bond.

damage If you deny it, let the danger° light

Upon your charter and your city's freedom.

You'll ask me why I rather choose to have   40

dead A weight of carrion° flesh than to receive

Three thousand ducats. I'll not answer that,

desire; whim But say it is my humor.° Is it answered?

What if my house be troubled with a rat,

And I be pleased to give ten thousand ducats   45

poisoned To have it baned?° What, are you answered yet?

Some men there are love not a gaping pig,[8]

Some that are mad if they behold a cat,

And others, when the bagpipe sings i' th' nose,[9]

1   *affection / Masters oft passion*

     **I.e., our instinctive reaction toward
     something often determines how
     we value it.**

2   *of force / Must yield to such inevitable
     shame / As to offend, himself being
     offended*

     **Cannot help running the risk of
     offending someone (by urinating
     uncontrollably—see line 50),
     having been himself offended
     (by the sound of the bagpipe)**

3   *main flood*

     I.e., high tide

4   *use question with*

     Pose the question to

Cannot contain their urine. For affection 50
Masters oft passion,[1] sways it to the mood
Of what it likes or loathes. Now, for your answer:

offered   As there is no firm reason to be rendered°

i.e., one man   Why he° cannot abide a gaping pig,

i.e., another   Why he,° a harmless necessary cat, 55

i.e., still another   Why he,° a woolen bagpipe, but of force

Must yield to such inevitable shame
As to offend, himself being offended,[2]
So can I give no reason, nor I will not,

fixed   More than a lodged° hate and a certain loathing 60

I bear Antonio, that I follow thus

unprofitable   A losing° suit against him. Are you answered?

Bassanio

This is no answer, thou unfeeling man,

course   To excuse the current° of thy cruelty.

Shylock

I am not bound to please thee with my answers. 65

Bassanio

Do all men kill the things they do not love?

Shylock

Hates any man the thing he would not kill?

Bassanio

Every offense is not a hate at first.

Shylock

What, wouldst thou have a serpent sting thee twice?

Antonio

can dispute   [to **Bassanio**] I pray you, think you question° with the
Jew? 70

You may as well go stand upon the beach

reduce   And bid the main flood[3] bate° his usual height.

You may as well use question with[4] the wolf
Why he hath made the ewe bleat for the lamb.

1   *brief and plain conveniency*

     Appropriate speed and directness

2   *purchased slave*

     **Both Venice and England were
     beneficiaries of the growing slave
     trade in the late 16th century, and
     Venice was an important slave
     market during this period.**

3   *such viands*

     I.e. the same food as you eat

4   *stand for*

     **Both "demand" and "represent" (as
     at line 142); cf. 3.2.57.**

You may as well forbid the mountain pines   75
wave   To wag° their high tops and to make no noise
agitated   When they are fretten° with the gusts of Heaven.
                  You may as well do anything most hard
compared to   As seek to soften that—than° which, what's harder?—
                  His Jewish heart. Therefore I do beseech you   80
                  Make no more offers, use no farther means,
                  But with all brief and plain conveniency¹
                  Let me have judgment and the Jew his will.

Bassanio

[*to* **Shylock**] For thy three thousand ducats, here is six.

Shylock

                  If every ducat in six thousand ducats   85
                  Were in six parts, and every part a ducat,
accept   I would not draw° them. I would have my bond.

Duke

offering   How shalt thou hope for mercy, rend'ring° none?

Shylock

                  What judgment shall I dread, doing no wrong?
                  You have among you many a purchased slave,²   90
                  Which, like your asses and your dogs and mules,
degrading / tasks You use in abject° and in slavish parts°
                  Because you bought them. Shall I say to you,
                  "Let them be free! Marry them to your heirs.
                  Why sweat they under burdens? Let their beds   95
                  Be made as soft as yours and let their palates
                  Be seasoned with such viands"?³ You will answer,
                  "The slaves are ours." So do I answer you.
                  The pound of flesh which I demand of him
expensively   Is dearly° bought. 'Tis mine, and I will have it.   100
                  If you deny me, fie upon your law;
                  There is no force in the decrees of Venice.
                  I stand for⁴ judgment. Answer. Shall I have it?

1   *stays without*

     Waits outside

2   *tainted wether*

     Literally, a sick castrated ram

Duke

In accordance with   Upon° my power I may dismiss this court,

Unless Bellario, a learnèd doctor,   105

resolve   Whom I have sent for to determine° this,

Come here today.

Salerio

My lord, here stays without¹

A messenger with letters from the doctor,

New come from Padua.

Duke

Bring us the letters. Call the messenger. [**Salerio** exits.]   110

Bassanio

Good cheer, Antonio! What, man, courage yet!

The Jew shall have my flesh, blood, bones, and all,

Before   Ere° thou shalt lose for me one drop of blood.

Antonio

I am a tainted wether² of the flock,

Most suited   Meetest° for death. The weakest kind of fruit   115

Drops earliest to the ground, and so let me.

You cannot better be employed, Bassanio,

Than to live still and write mine epitaph.

Enter **Nerissa** [disguised as a law clerk].

Duke

Came you from Padua, from Bellario?

Nerissa

From both, my lord. Bellario greets your Grace.   120

[hands the **Duke** a letter]

[**Shylock** sharpens a knife on the bottom of his shoe.]

Bassanio

sharpen   Why dost thou whet° thy knife so earnestly?

1   *for thy life let justice be accused*

    **I.e., let justice be blamed for
    permitting you to live.**

2   *To hold opinion with Pythagoras*

    **To agree with Pythagoras (a Greek
    philosopher who believed that the
    soul was immortal and "transmi-
    grated," i.e., transferred itself,
    from one living form to another)**

3   *Even from the gallows did his fell soul
    fleet, / And, whilst thou layest in thy
    unhallowed dam, / Infused itself in thee*

    **While still on the gallows, its savage
    (*fell*) soul drifted away, and while
    you were in your damned mother's
    womb, it lodged inside you.**

4   *rail*

    I.e., remove (by berating me)

5   *but offend'st*

    Only damage

Shylock

To cut the forfeiture from that bankrupt there.

Gratiano

Not on thy sole, but on thy soul, harsh Jew,

sharp Thou mak'st thy knife keen.° But no metal can—

i.e., executioner's No, not the hangman's° axe—bear half the keenness 125

malice Of thy sharp envy.° Can no prayers pierce thee?

Shylock

No, none that thou hast wit enough to make.

Gratiano

most detestable Oh, be thou damned, inexecrable° dog,

And for thy life let justice be accused![1]

Thou almost mak'st me waver in my faith

To hold opinion with Pythagoras[2] 130

That souls of animals infuse themselves

bodies / i.e., vicious Into the trunks° of men. Thy currish° spirit

Governed a wolf who, hanged for human slaughter,

Even from the gallows did his fell soul fleet, 135

And, whilst thou layest in thy unhallowed dam,

Infused itself in thee,[3] for thy desires

Are wolvish, bloody, starved, and ravenous.

Shylock

Till thou canst rail[4] the seal from off my bond,

Thou but offend'st[5] thy lungs to speak so loud. 140

Repair thy wit, good youth, or it will fall

To cureless ruin. I stand here for law.

Duke

recommend; introduce This letter from Bellario doth commend°

A young and learnèd doctor to our court.

Where is he?

Nerissa

very near He attendeth here hard° by 145

To know your answer whether you'll admit him.

1   *turned o'er*

    Read through; pored over

2   *at my importunity to fill up your Grace's*
    request in my stead

    At my urging, to respond to your
    summons instead of me

3   *let his lack of years be no impediment to*
    let him lack a reverend estimation

    I.e., do not let his youth deprive
    him of your high esteem.

4   *whose trial shall better publish his*
    commendation

    The testing of whom will demon-
    strate his worth more (than my
    words)

5   *holds the present question*

    Is now being examined

Duke

With all my heart.—Some three or four of you

escort Go give him courteous conduct° to this place.

[*Attendants exit.*]

Meantime the court shall hear Bellario's letter.

[*reads*] "Your Grace shall understand that at the receipt   150

of your letter I am very sick, but in the instant that

your messenger came, in loving visitation was with

me a young doctor of Rome. His name is Balthazar.

I acquainted him with the cause in controversy be-

tween the Jew and Antonio the merchant. We turned   155

o'er¹ many books together. He is furnished with my

improved opinion, which, bettered° with his own learning, the

greatness whereof I cannot enough commend, comes

with him at my importunity to fill up your Grace's re-

quest in my stead.² I beseech you, let his lack of years   160

be no impediment to let him lack a reverend estima-

tion,³ for I never knew so young a body with so old a

head. I leave him to your gracious acceptance, whose

trial shall better publish his commendation."⁴

i.e., disguised as   *Enter* **Portia** *for°* *Balthazar.*

You hear the learned Bellario, what he writes,   165

And here I take it is the doctor come.

—Give me your hand. Come you from old Bellario?

Portia

I did, my lord.

Duke

You are welcome. Take your place.

dispute Are you acquainted with the difference°

That holds this present question⁵ in the court?   170

1   *in such rule*

So proper; in such accordance with
our procedures

2   *gentle rain*

See Ecclesiasticus 35:19(26): "Oh,
how fair a thing is mercy in time
of anguish and trouble! It is like a
cloud of rain, that cometh in the
time of a drought" and Deuterono-
my 32:2: "My doctrine shall drip as
the rain and my speech shall distill
as doth the dew, as the shower
upon the herbs and the rain upon
the grass."

Portia

thoroughly I am informèd throughly° of the cause.

Which is the merchant here, and which the Jew?

Duke

Antonio and old Shylock, both stand forth.

Portia

Is your name Shylock?

Shylock

Shylock is my name.

Portia

lawsuit Of a strange nature is the suit° you follow,   175

Yet in such rule¹ that the Venetian law

find fault with Cannot impugn° you as you do proceed.

power [*to* **Antonio**] You stand within his danger,° do you not?

Antonio

Ay, so he says.

Portia

Do you confess the bond?

Antonio

I do.

Portia

Then must the Jew be merciful.   180

Shylock

On what compulsion must I? Tell me that.

Portia

compelled The quality of mercy is not strained.°

It droppeth as the gentle rain² from Heaven

Upon the place beneath. It is twice blessed:

It blesseth him that gives and him that takes.   185

graces; befits 'Tis mightiest in the mightiest. It becomes°

The thronèd monarch better than his crown.

1 *We do pray for mercy, / And that same prayer doth teach us all to render / The deeds of mercy.*

The reference is to the Lord's Prayer, which asks God to "forgive us our debts, as we also forgive our debtors" (Matthew 6:12); see also Ecclesiasticus 28:2: "Forgive thy neighbour the hurt that he hath done unto thee, so shall thy sins also be forgiven when thou prayest."

2 *give sentence 'gainst*

Rule against

3 *My deeds upon my head.*

I am willing to accept the consequences of my own actions.

4 *bears down*

Overwhelms

5 *Wrest once the law to your authority*

Just once, use your power to bend the law.

earthly His scepter shows the force of temporal° power,

of The attribute to° awe and majesty

Wherein doth sit the dread and fear of kings;   190

power But mercy is above this sceptered sway.°

It is enthronèd in the hearts of kings.

It is an attribute to God himself,

most like And earthly power doth then show likest° God's

tempers When mercy seasons° justice. Therefore, Jew,   195

Though justice be thy plea, consider this:

path; process That in the course° of justice none of us

Should see salvation. We do pray for mercy,

And that same prayer doth teach us all to render

The deeds of mercy.[1] I have spoke thus much   200

temper; moderate To mitigate° the justice of thy plea,

Which if thou follow, this strict court of Venice

Must needs give sentence 'gainst[2] the merchant there.

Shylock

My deeds upon my head.[3] I crave the law,

The penalty, and forfeit of my bond.   205

Portia

repay Is he not able to discharge° the money?

Bassanio

offer Yes, here I tender° it for him in the court—

Yea, twice the sum. If that will not suffice,

I will be bound to pay it ten times o'er,

On forfeit of my hands, my head, my heart.   210

If this will not suffice, it must appear

That malice bears down[4] truth. [*to* **Duke**] And I
     beseech you,

Wrest once the law to your authority.[5]

To do a great right, do a little wrong,

And curb this cruel devil of his will.   215

1   *Venice*

Venice was a republic, not a
monarchy, and was famed for its
"inexorable administration of
justice." (Brown, see For Further
Reading, cites Z. S. Fink, *Classical
Republicans* [1945], p. 43.)

2   *A Daniel come to judgment, yea, a Daniel!*

An allusion to a story from the
Apocrypha, in which the young
Daniel judges in favor of Susanna,
who had been falsely accused of
unchastity by the Elders. See also
Ezekiel 28:3: "Behold, thou thinkest
thyself wiser than Daniel."

Portia

It must not be. There is no power in Venice[1]
Can alter a decree establishèd.
'Twill be recorded for a precedent,
And many an error by the same example
Will rush into the state. It cannot be.   220

Shylock

A Daniel come to judgment, yea, a Daniel![2]
—O wise young judge, how I do honor thee!

Portia

I pray you, let me look upon the bond.

Shylock

Here 'tis, most reverend doctor; here it is.

                                        [hands her a paper]

Portia

Shylock, there's thrice thy money offered thee.   225

Shylock

An oath, an oath, I have an oath in Heaven.
Shall I lay perjury upon my soul?
No, not for Venice.

Portia

                            Why, this bond is forfeit.
And lawfully by this the Jew may claim
A pound of flesh to be by him cut off   230
Nearest the merchant's heart.—Be merciful.
Take thrice thy money. Bid me tear the bond.

Shylock

exact terms   When it is paid according to the tenor.°
It doth appear you are a worthy judge.
explanation   You know the law. Your exposition°   235
Hath been most sound. I charge you by the law,
Whereof you are a well-deserving pillar,
Proceed to judgment. By my soul I swear

1   *I stay here on my bond.*

I.e., I insist on the original terms of
the agreement.

2   *Hath full relation to*

Fully authorizes

There is no power in the tongue of man
To alter me. I stay here on my bond. ¹ 240

Antonio

Most heartily I do beseech the court
To give the judgment.

Portia

Why then, thus it is:
You must prepare your bosom for his knife.

Shylock

O noble judge! O excellent young man!

Portia

For the intent and purpose of the law 245
Hath full relation to ² the penalty,
Which here appeareth due upon the bond.

Shylock

'Tis very true. O wise and upright judge!
How much more elder art thou than thy looks.

Portia

[*to* **Antonio**] Therefore lay bare your bosom.

Shylock

Ay, his breast. 250
So says the bond. Doth it not, noble judge?
"Nearest his heart"—those are the very words.

Portia

scales   It is so. Are there balance° here to weigh
The flesh?

Shylock

I have them ready.

Portia

nearby / expense   Have by° some surgeon, Shylock, on your charge,° 255
To stop his wounds lest he do bleed to death.

Shylock

stipulated   Is it so nominated° in the bond?

1   *Speak me fair*

    Speak well of me

2   *Repent but you*

    Regret only

Portia

It is not so expressed, but what of that?

'Twere good you do so much for charity.

Shylock

I cannot find it. 'Tis not in the bond.   260

Portia

[*to* **Antonio**] You, merchant, have you anything to say?

Antonio

mentally fortified But little. I am armed° and well prepared.

—Give me your hand, Bassanio. Fare you well.

Grieve not that I am fall'n to this for you,

For herein fortune shows herself more kind   265

always / habit Than is her custom. It is still° her use°

To let the wretched man outlive his wealth,

To view with hollow eye and wrinkled brow

that An age of poverty, from which° ling'ring penance

Of such misery doth she cut me off.   270

Commend me to your honorable wife.

manner Tell her the process° of Antonio's end.

Say how I loved you. Speak me fair¹ in death,

And when the tale is told, bid her be judge

Whether Bassanio had not once a love.   275

Repent but you² that you shall lose your friend,

And he repents not that he pays your debt.

For if the Jew do cut but deep enough,

I'll pay it instantly with all my heart.

Bassanio

Antonio, I am married to a wife   280

Who Which° is as dear to me as life itself;

But life itself, my wife, and all the world

valued Are not with me esteemed° above thy life.

I would lose all—ay, sacrifice them all

release Here to this devil—to deliver° you.   285

1   *any of the stock of Barabbas*

Any son of Barabbas (the thief whom Pilate pardoned instead of Jesus at the request of the people in Luke 23, and also the name of the main character in Marlowe's *The Jew of Malta*)

Portia

Your wife would give you little thanks for that

nearby If she were by° to hear you make the offer.

Gratiano

I have a wife, who I protest I love.

I would she were in Heaven, so she could

heavenly being Entreat some power° to change this currish Jew.   290

Nerissa

'Tis well you offer it behind her back.

(it) otherwise The wish would make else° an unquiet house.

Shylock

These be the Christian husbands. I have a daughter.

I wish Would° any of the stock of Barabbas'

Had been her husband rather than a Christian!   295

waste / proceed with —We trifle° time. I pray thee, pursue° sentence.

Portia

A pound of that same merchant's flesh is thine.

The court awards it, and the law doth give it.

Shylock

Most rightful judge!

Portia

And you must cut this flesh from off his breast.   300

The law allows it, and the court awards it.

Shylock

Most learnèd judge, a sentence! Come; prepare.

Portia

Tarry a little. There is something else.

This bond doth give thee here no jot of blood.

explicitly The words expressly° are "a pound of flesh."   305

Take then thy bond, take thou thy pound of flesh,

But in the cutting it if thou dost shed

One drop of Christian blood, thy lands and goods

1   *be it but so much / As makes it light or*

     heavy in the substance

     **I.e., even if it is enough to make
     only the slightest difference in the
     gross weight**

2   *scruple*

     **A very small measurement of
     weight (one twenty-fourth of an
     ounce)**

confiscated Are by the laws of Venice confiscate°
Unto the state of Venice.   310

Gratiano

Take note O upright judge! Mark,° Jew! O learnèd judge!

Shylock

Is that the law?

Portia

decree   Thyself shalt see the act,°
For as thou urgest justice, be assured
Thou shalt have justice more than thou desir'st.

Gratiano

O learnèd judge! Mark, Jew, a learnèd judge!   315

Shylock

I take this offer then: pay the bond thrice
And let the Christian go.

Bassanio

               Here is the money.

Portia

Wait Soft!° The Jew shall have all justice. Soft; no haste.
He shall have nothing but the penalty.

Gratiano

O Jew! An upright judge, a learnèd judge!   320

Portia

Therefore prepare thee to cut off the flesh.
Shed thou no blood, nor cut thou less nor more

exactly But just° a pound of flesh. If thou tak'st more
exact Or less than a just° pound, be it but so much
As makes it light or heavy in the substance¹   325

fraction Or the division° of the twentieth part
move Of one poor scruple²—nay, if the scale do turn°
Even / amount But° in the estimation° of a hair—
Thou diest, and all thy goods are confiscate.

1   *I have you on the hip*

I.e., I have the advantage (a term from wrestling; the phrase also appears in 1.3.42)

2   *barely my principal*

Even the amount of the original loan

3   *privy coffer*

Treasury

Gratiano

A second Daniel! A Daniel, Jew!   330

Now, infidel, I have you on the hip. [1]

Portia

Why doth the Jew pause? Take thy forfeiture.

Shylock

Give me my principal and let me go.

Bassanio

I have it ready for thee. Here it is.

Portia

He hath refused it in the open court.   335

He shall have merely° justice and his bond.   *absolute*

Gratiano

A Daniel, still say I, a second Daniel!

—I thank thee, Jew, for teaching me that word.

Shylock

Shall I not have barely my principal? [2]

Portia

Thou shalt have nothing but the forfeiture, °   340

To be so taken at thy peril, Jew.   *i.e., Antonio's flesh*

Shylock

Why then, the devil give him good of it!

I'll stay no longer question. °   *to argue my case*   [*begins to exit*]

Portia

Tarry, Jew.

The law hath yet another hold on you.

It is enacted in the laws of Venice,   345

If it be proved against an alien°   *foreigner*

That by direct or indirect attempts

He seek the life of any citizen,

The party 'gainst the which he doth contrive°   *plot*

Shall seize one half his goods. The other half   350

Comes to the privy coffer [3] of the state,

1   *in the mercy / Of the Duke only, 'gainst all*
    other voice

    **Completely in the Duke's hands,
    without any possibility of appeal**

2   *by manifest proceeding*

    As can be obviously seen

3   *The danger formerly by me rehearsed*

    **The punishment I have just
    described to you**

4   *Which humbleness may drive unto a fine*

    **Which, if you display humility, may
    be commuted to a *fine* (rather than
    the wholesale forfeiture of your
    wealth)**

5   *for the state, not for Antonio*

    **Portia explains that only the half of
    Shylock's goods taken for *the state*
    may be reduced to a fine; Antonio
    will keep that half that he has been
    given.**

6   *A halter gratis*

    A noose, for free

And the offender's life lies in the mercy
Of the Duke only, 'gainst all other voice.[1]
In which predicament I say thou stand'st,
For it appears by manifest proceeding[2]   355
That indirectly—and directly too—
Thou hast contrived against the very life
Of the defendant, and thou hast incurred
The danger formerly by me rehearsed.[3]
Down, therefore, and beg mercy of the Duke.   360

Gratiano

permission   Beg that thou mayst have leave° to hang thyself,
And yet, thy wealth being forfeit to the state,
still remaining / rope   Thou hast not left° the value of a cord.°
expense   Therefore thou must be hanged at the state's charge.°

Duke

That thou shalt see the difference of our spirit,   365
I pardon thee thy life before thou ask it.
For half thy wealth, it is Antonio's;
The other half comes to the general state,
Which humbleness may drive unto a fine.[4]

Portia

Ay, for the state, not for Antonio.[5]   370

Shylock

Nay, take my life and all. Pardon not that.
support   You take my house when you do take the prop°
That doth sustain my house. You take my life
When you do take the means whereby I live.

Portia

What mercy can you render him, Antonio?   375

Gratiano

A halter gratis,[6] nothing else, for God's sake.

1   *of all he dies possessed*

**Of everything he possesses at the
time of his death**

2   *thou shouldst have had ten more*

I.e., you would have twelve *god-
fathers* **(the number of a full jury)
to answer to.**

Antonio

So please my lord the Duke and all the court,

cancel To quit° the fine for one half of his goods

so long as I am content, so° he will let me have

trust The other half in use° to render it   380

Upon his death unto the gentleman

That lately stole his daughter.

Two things provided more: that for this favor

immediately He presently° become a Christian;

The other, that he do record a gift,   385

Here in the court, of all he dies possessed,[1]

son-in-law Unto his son° Lorenzo and his daughter.

Duke

withdraw He shall do this, or else I do recant°

The pardon that I late pronouncèd here.

Portia

Art thou contented, Jew? What dost thou say?   390

Shylock

I am content.

Portia

draw up [*to* **Nerissa**] Clerk, draw° a deed of gift.

Shylock

I pray you, give me leave to go from hence.

I am not well. Send the deed after me,

And I will sign it.

Duke

Get thee gone, but do it.   395

Gratiano

[*to* **Shylock**] In christ'ning shalt thou have two god-
        fathers.

Had I been judge, thou shouldst have had ten more,[2]

christening basin To bring thee to the gallows, not to the font.°

                            [**Shylock**] *exits.*

1   *your leisure serves you not*

That you don't have time

2   *cope your courteous pains withal*

Give in return for your generous
efforts

3   *over and above*

I.e., beyond the 3,000 ducats

4   *attempt you further*

I.e., try again to pay you

5   *pardon me*

Forgive me (for urging you so
forcefully)

Duke

[*to* **Portia**] Sir, I entreat you home with me to dinner.

Portia

for   I humbly do desire your Grace of° pardon.   400

I must away this night toward Padua,

fitting   And it is meet° I presently set forth.

Duke

I am sorry that your leisure serves you not. [1]

reward —Antonio, gratify° this gentleman,

For in my mind you are much bound to him.   405

                                              Duke *and his train exit.*

Bassanio

[*to* **Portia**] Most worthy gentleman, I and my friend

Have by your wisdom been this day acquitted

Of grievous penalties, in lieu whereof

Three thousand ducats due unto the Jew

repay   We freely cope° your courteous pains withal. [2]   410

Antonio

And stand indebted, over and above, [3]

In love and service to you evermore.

Portia

He is well paid that is well satisfied,

And I, delivering you, am satisfied,

consider And therein do account° myself well paid.   415

My mind was never yet more mercenary.

remember I pray you, know° me when we meet again.

I wish you well, and so I take my leave.   [*begins to exit*]

Bassanio

necessity Dear sir, of force° I must attempt you further. [4]

Take some remembrance of us as a tribute,   420

Not as fee. Grant me two things, I pray you:

Not to deny me, and to pardon me. [5]

1   *press me far*

    Continue to insist

2   *I have a mind to it*

    I.e., I very much want it.

3   *There's more depends on this than on the
    value.*

    **This (ring) is worth more than its
    monetary value.**

4   *An if*

    If

Portia

You press me far,¹ and therefore I will yield.

[*to* **Antonio**] Give me your gloves; I'll wear them for
     your sake.

[*to* **Bassanio**] And for your love, I'll take this ring from you.   425

Do not draw back your hand. I'll take no more,

And you in love shall not deny me this.

Bassanio

This ring, good sir? Alas, it is a trifle.

I will not shame myself to give you this.

Portia

I will have nothing else but only this.   430

And now methinks I have a mind to it.²

Bassanio

There's more depends on this than on the value.³

most expensive   The dearest° ring in Venice will I give you,

And find it out by proclamation.

Only for this, I pray you, pardon me.   435

Portia

generous   I see, sir, you are liberal° in offers.

You taught me first to beg, and now methinks

You teach me how a beggar should be answered.

Bassanio

Good sir, this ring was given me by my wife,

And, when she put it on, she made me vow   440

That I should neither sell nor give nor lose it.

Portia

excuse / allows   That 'scuse° serves° many men to save their gifts.

An if⁴ your wife be not a madwoman,

And know how well I have deserved this ring,

She would not hold out enemy forever   445

For giving it to me. Well, peace be with you.

                              [**Portia** *and* **Nerissa**] *exit.*

1   *thither*

Go there (i.e., Antonio's house)

Antonio

My Lord Bassanio, let him have the ring.

in addition Let his deservings and my love withal°

Be valued 'gainst your wife's commandment.

Bassanio

Go, Gratiano; run and overtake him. 450

Give him the ring and bring him, if thou canst,

Unto Antonio's house. Away; make haste.

Gratiano exits.

Come; you and I will thither¹ presently.

And in the morning early will we both

Hurry Fly° toward Belmont. Come, Antonio. *They exit.* 455

1   *you are well o'erta'en*

I am glad I have caught you.

Act 4, Scene 2

*Enter [**Portia** and] **Nerissa** [still disguised].*

Portia

contract   Inquire the Jew's house out. Give him this deed°
And let him sign it. We'll away tonight
And be a day before our husbands home.
This deed will be well welcome to Lorenzo.

*Enter **Gratiano**.*

Gratiano

Fair sir, you are well o'erta'en.'   5

consideration   My Lord Bassanio upon more advice°

request   Hath sent you here this ring and doth entreat°
Your company at dinner.   [*hands her a ring*]

Portia

                 That cannot be.
His ring I do accept most thankfully,
And so I pray you tell him. Furthermore,   10
I pray you show my youth old Shylock's house.

Gratiano

That will I do.

Nerissa

         [*to **Portia**] Sir, I would speak with you.
[*aside to **Portia**] I'll see if I can get my husband's ring,
Which I did make him swear to keep forever.

Portia

[*aside to **Nerissa**] Thou mayst, I warrant. We shall have

much   old° swearing   15
That they did give the rings away to men.

1   *outface them*

Stare them down; stand up to them

But we'll outface them ' and outswear them too.
Away; make haste. Thou know'st where I will tarry.

[*She exits.*]

Nerissa

[*to* **Gratiano**] Come, good sir. Will you show me to this
house?   [*They exit.*]   20

1   *Troilus*

Troilus was a Trojan prince in love
with Cressida. During the Trojan
War, she was sent to the Greeks
in exchange for a Trojan officer
and soon became the mistress of
Diomedes. Shakespeare's account
is based on Chaucer's *Troilus and
Criseyde*, 5, 647–667.

2   *Thisbe*

In Chaucer's *Legend of Good Women*,
Thisbe, going to meet her lover
Pyramus, is frightened away by
a lion. When Pyramus arrives he
finds her scarf and, thinking she
has been killed, commits suicide;
Thisbe kills herself when she
returns and finds Pyramus's body.
Shakespeare provides a comic
version of the story in Act 5 of *A
Midsummer Night's Dream*.

3   *ere himself*

I.e., before (she saw) the lion itself

4   *Dido*

In Virgil's *Aeneid*, Dido, Queen of
Carthage, falls in love with Aeneas
and commits suicide when he abandons her to found the city of Rome.
Chaucer includes Dido in his *Legend
of Good Women*.

5   *Medea*

In book 5 of Ovid's *Metamorphoses*,
the sorceress Medea (who helped
her lover Jason win the golden

fleece) concocts a potion that
makes Aeson, Jason's father, young
again. Later, Jason abandons
Medea for another woman, and she
kills their children for revenge.

6   *steal*

Escape (but inevitably also with the
sense "rob," as also in *stealing* in
line 19, reinforcing the tragic impli-
cations of all the lovers' stories)

7   *unthrift*

Extravagant (in opposition to her
father's *thrifty mind* at 2.5.53)

Act 5, Scene 1

Enter **Lorenzo** *and* **Jessica**.

Lorenzo
The moon shines bright. In such a night as this,
When the sweet wind did gently kiss the trees,
And they did make no noise, in such a night
Troilus,[1] methinks, mounted the Trojan walls
And sighed his soul toward the Grecian tents   5
Where Cressid lay that night.

Jessica
                     In such a night

skip over / dewy grass   Did Thisbe[2] fearfully o'ertrip° the dew°
And saw the lion's shadow ere himself[3]
in fear   And ran dismayed° away.

Lorenzo
                In such a night
Stood Dido[4] with a willow in her hand   10
beckoned   Upon the wild sea banks, and waft° her love
To come again to Carthage.

Jessica
               In such a night
Medea[5] gathered the enchanted herbs
That did renew old Aeson.

Lorenzo
              In such a night
Did Jessica steal[6] from the wealthy Jew,   15
And with an unthrift[7] love did run from Venice
As far as Belmont.

Jessica
            In such a night
Did young Lorenzo swear he loved her well,

1   *I would outnight you, did nobody come*

**I.e., I would outdo you in recalling
these legendary nights, if no one
would interrupt us.**

2   *nor we have not heard from him*

Nor have we heard from him

Stealing her soul with many vows of faith,
And ne'er a true one.

Lorenzo

In such a night   20

ill-tempered woman Did pretty Jessica, like a little shrew,°

Slander her love, and he forgave it her.

Jessica

I would outnight you, did nobody come,¹

footsteps But, hark, I hear the footing° of a man.

*Enter [**Stephano**,] a messenger.*

Lorenzo

Who comes so fast in silence of the night?   25

Stephano

A friend.

Lorenzo

A friend? What friend? Your name, I pray you, friend?

Stephano

Stephano is my name, and I bring word

My mistress will before the break of day

wander Be here at Belmont. She doth stray° about   30

roadside shrines By holy crosses,° where she kneels and prays

For happy wedlock hours.

Lorenzo

Who comes with her?

Stephano

None but a holy hermit and her maid.

I pray you, is my master yet returned?

Lorenzo

He is not, nor we have not heard from him.²   35

—But go we in, I pray thee, Jessica,

1   *Sola, sola!*

     **Launcelot imitates the horn used
     to announce the arrival of a mes-
     senger.**

2   *Wo, ha, ho!*

     A falconer's call

3   *Leave holloaing*

     Stop shouting.

4   *your music forth into the air*

     Your musicians outside

And ceremoniously let us prepare
Some welcome for the mistress of the house.

Enter [**Launcelot** *the*] *clown.*

Launcelot
Sola, sola!¹ Wo, ha, ho!² Sola, sola!
Lorenzo
Who calls?   40
Launcelot
Sola! Did you see Master Lorenzo? Master Lorenzo,
sola, sola!
Lorenzo
Leave holloaing,³ man. Here.
Launcelot
Sola! Where, where?
Lorenzo
Here.   45
Launcelot
messenger   Tell him there's a post° come from my master with his
before   horn full of good news. My master will be here ere°
morning.   [**Launcelot** *exits.*]
Lorenzo
await   Sweet soul, let's in and there expect° their coming.
And yet, no matter. Why should we go in?   50
announce   —My friend Stephano, signify,° I pray you,
Within the house, your mistress is at hand.
And bring your music forth into the air.⁴
[**Stephano** *exits.*]
How sweet the moonlight sleeps upon this bank.
Here will we sit and let the sounds of music   55
Creep in our ears. Soft stillness and the night
Suit/notes   Become° the touches° of sweet harmony.

1   *patens*

Small plates or disks (i.e., the stars)

2   *But in his motion like an angel sings*

That does not sing like an angel as it
moves. It was widely believed that
stars and planets, while moving
in their fixed spheres, produced
harmonious music inaudible to
humans.

3   *Still choiring to the young-eyed cherubins*

Always singing to the attentive an-
gels (*cherubins* is an irregular plural
of "cherub")

4   *Such harmony is in immortal souls, / But
whilst this muddy vesture of decay / Doth
grossly close it in, we cannot hear it.*

I.e., our immortal souls produce a
similar sound, but, as long as they
are trapped in our physical bodies,
we cannot hear it.

5   *Diana*

The Roman goddess of the moon
and of chastity

6   *Fetching mad bounds*

Leaping wildly

7   *make a mutual stand*

All stop simultaneously

8   *the poet*

I.e., Ovid, who includes the story
of Orpheus in his *Metamorphoses*
(Book 12)

Sit, Jessica. Look how the floor of Heaven
Is thick inlaid with patens[1] of bright gold.
There's not the smallest orb which thou behold'st   60
But in his motion like an angel sings,[2]
Still choiring to the young-eyed cherubins.[3]
Such harmony is in immortal souls,
But whilst this muddy vesture of decay
Doth grossly close it in, we cannot hear it.[4]   65

[Enter musicians.]

Come, ho, and wake Diana[5] with a hymn!
notes / i.e., Portia's   With sweetest touches° pierce your mistress'° ear
And draw her home with music.

                                    [They] play music.

Jessica
I am never merry when I hear sweet music.
Lorenzo
preoccupied   The reason is your spirits are attentive.°   70
if you   For do° but note a wild and wanton herd
group / untamed   Or race° of youthful and unhandled° colts
Fetching mad bounds,[6] bellowing and neighing loud,
Which is the hot condition of their blood,
If they but hear perchance a trumpet sound,   75
Or any air of music touch their ears,
You shall perceive them make a mutual stand,[7]
Their savage eyes turned to a modest gaze
By the sweet power of music. Therefore the poet[8]
invent / attracted   Did feign° that Orpheus drew° trees, stones, and floods   80
nothing / unfeeling   Since naught° so stockish,° hard, and full of rage,
moment / its   But music for the time° doth change his° nature.
The man that hath no music in himself,
harmony   Nor is not moved with concord° of sweet sounds,

1   *Erebus*

     A dark region of the underworld

2   *his state*

     I.e., the substitute's grandeur

3   *the main of waters*

     I.e., the ocean

4   *without respect*

     Except in relation to something else

plots / plunder   Is fit for treasons, stratagems,° and spoils.°   85
                     The motions of his spirit are dull as night,
inclinations   And his affections° dark as Erebus.¹
                     Let no such man be trusted. Mark the music.

Enter **Portia** *and* **Nerissa**.

Portia
That light we see is burning in my hall.
How far that little candle throws his beams!   90
wicked   So shines a good deed in a naughty° world.
Nerissa
When the moon shone we did not see the candle.
Portia
So doth the greater glory dim the less.
deputy   A substitute° shines brightly as a king
nearby   Until a king be by,° and then his state²   95
               Empties itself, as doth an inland brook
               Into the main of waters.³ Music, hark.
Nerissa
It is your music, madam, of the house.
Portia
Nothing is good, I see, without respect.⁴
Methinks it sounds much sweeter than by day.   100
Nerissa
Silence bestows that virtue on it, madam.
Portia
The crow doth sing as sweetly as the lark
listened to   When neither is attended,° and I think
                The nightingale, if she should sing by day
                When every goose is cackling, would be thought   105
                No better a musician than the wren.

1   *by season seasoned are*

By appearing at an opportune time
are raised

2   *Endymion*

In classical mythology, a shepherd
with whom Diana, the goddess of
the moon, fell in love and caused to
sleep forever so she could visit him
whenever she pleased.

How many things by season seasoned are[1]
To their right praise and true perfection!
Quiet Peace!° How the moon sleeps with Endymion[2]
And would not be awaked. *[Music stops.]*

Lorenzo

That is the voice,   110
Or I am much deceived, of Portia.

Portia

He knows me as the blind man knows the cuckoo—
By the bad voice.

Lorenzo

Dear lady, welcome home.

Portia

We have been praying for our husbands' welfare,
prospers / prayers Which speed,° we hope, the better for our words.°   115
Are they returned?

Lorenzo

Madam, they are not yet,
in advance But there is come a messenger before°
To signify their coming.

Portia

Go in, Nerissa.
Give order to my servants that they take
from here No note at all of our being absent hence.°   120
—Nor you, Lorenzo.—Jessica, nor you.

[Trumpet sounds.]

Lorenzo

Your husband is at hand. I hear his trumpet.
We are no tell-tales, madam. Fear you not.

Portia

This night methinks is but the daylight sick.
It looks a little paler. 'Tis a day   125
Such as the day is when the sun is hid.

1   *We should hold day with the Antipodes, /*
    If you would walk in absence of the sun.

    **We would have daylight, as they do
    on the other side of the Earth (*the
    Antipodes*), if you would go out while
    it is night (because your beauty is
    so radiant).**

2   *acquitted of*

    (1) repaid for; (2) released from

3   *I scant this breathing courtesy*

    **I cut short this (merely) verbal
    welcome.**

Enter **Bassanio, Antonio, Gratiano,** *and their followers.* [**Gratiano** *and* **Nerissa** *move aside and talk.*]

Bassanio

[*to* **Portia**] We should hold day with the Antipodes,
If you would walk in absence of the sun.[1]

Portia

unchaste — Let me give light, but let me not be light,°
sad — For a light wife doth make a heavy° husband, — 130
And never be Bassanio so for me.
arrange; determine — But God sort° all! You are welcome home, my lord.

Bassanio

I thank you, madam. Give welcome to my friend.
This is the man, this is Antonio,
To whom I am so infinitely bound. — 135

Portia

every / obligated — You should in all° sense be much bound° to him,
For as I hear he was much bound for you.

Antonio

No more than I am well acquitted of.[2]

Portia

Sir, you are very welcome to our house.
be demonstrated — It must appear° in other ways than words; — 140
Therefore I scant this breathing courtesy.[3]

Gratiano

[*to* **Nerissa**] By yonder moon I swear you do me wrong.
In faith, I gave it to the judge's clerk.
gelded; castrated — Would he were gelt° that had it, for my part,
to — Since you do take it, love, so much at° heart. — 145

Portia

A quarrel, ho, already? What's the matter?

1   *cutler's poetry*

     I.e., insipid verse (the kind of in-
     scription one might find engraved
     on a knife blade; a *cutler* is someone
     who makes or sells knives)

2   *an if*

     If

Gratiano

About a hoop of gold, a paltry ring

inscription That she did give me, whose posy° was

For all the world like cutler's poetry¹

Upon a knife: "Love me and leave me not." 150

Nerissa

What talk you of the posy or the value?

You swore to me when I did give it you

That you would wear it till your hour of death,

And that it should lie with you in your grave.

If Though° not for me, yet for your vehement oaths, 155

careful You should have been respective° and have kept it.

Gave it a judge's clerk! No, God's my judge.

The clerk will ne'er wear hair on 's face that had it.

Gratiano

He will, an if² he live to be a man.

Nerissa

Ay, if a woman live to be a man. 160

Gratiano

Now, by this hand, I gave it to a youth,

stunted A kind of boy, a little scrubbèd° boy

No higher than thyself, the judge's clerk,

chattering A prating° boy that begged it as a fee.

I could not for my heart deny it him. 165

Portia

You were to blame, I must be plain with you,

carelessly To part so slightly° with your wife's first gift,

A thing stuck on with oaths upon your finger

And so riveted with faith unto your flesh.

I gave my love a ring and made him swear 170

Never to part with it, and here he stands.

I dare be sworn for him he would not leave it

Nor pluck it from his finger for the wealth

1   *I were best to*

      I.e., it would be best for me if I
      could

possesses   That the world masters.° Now in faith, Gratiano,

You give your wife too unkind a cause of grief.   175

If   An° 'twere to me, I should be mad at it.

Bassanio

[*aside*] Why, I were best to' cut my left hand off

And swear I lost the ring defending it.

Gratiano

My Lord Bassanio gave his ring away

Unto the judge that begged it and indeed   180

Deserved it too; and then the boy, his clerk,

That took some pains in writing, he begged mine,

anything   And neither man nor master would take aught°

But the two rings.

Portia

                                What ring gave you, my lord?

Not that, I hope, which you received of me.   185

Bassanio

If I could add a lie unto a fault

I would deny it, but you see my finger

Hath not the ring upon it. It is gone.

Portia

Even so void is your false heart of truth.

By Heaven, I will ne'er come in your bed   190

Until I see the ring.

Nerissa

                        [*to* **Gratiano**] Nor I in yours

Till I again see mine.

Bassanio

                        Sweet Portia,

If you did know to whom I gave the ring,

If you did know for whom I gave the ring,

understand   And would conceive° for what I gave the ring,   195

parted with   And how unwillingly I left° the ring

1 *wanted the modesty*

Would lack the considerateness

2 *ceremony*

Symbol of commitment

3 *I'll die for 't but*

I would bet my life that

4 *civil doctor*

Doctor of civil law

5 *these blessèd candles of the night*

I.e., the stars

6 *liberal*

Generous (but also with the sense
"lascivious")

When naught would be accepted but the ring,

diminish   You would abate° the strength of your displeasure.

Portia

power   If you had known the virtue° of the ring,

Or half her worthiness that gave the ring,   200

retain   Or your own honor to contain° the ring,

You would not then have parted with the ring.

What man is there so much unreasonable,

If you had pleased to have defended it

With any terms of zeal, wanted the modesty[1]   205

demand   To urge° the thing held as a ceremony?[2]

Nerissa teaches me what to believe:

was given   I'll die for 't but[3] some woman had° the ring.

Bassanio

No, by my honor, madam, by my soul,

No woman had it but a civil doctor,[4]   210

Who   Which° did refuse three thousand ducats of me

And begged the ring, the which I did deny him

allowed   And suffered° him to go displeased away—

Even he that had held up the very life

Of my dear friend. What should I say, sweet lady?   215

compelled   I was enforced° to send it after him.

beseiged   I was beset° with shame and courtesy.

My honor would not let ingratitude

i.e., my honor So much besmear it.° Pardon me, good lady,

For by these blessèd candles of the night,[5]   220

Had you been there I think you would have begged

The ring of me to give the worthy doctor.

Portia

Let not that doctor e'er come near my house!

Since he hath got the jewel that I loved,

And that which you did swear to keep for me,   225

I will become as liberal[6] as you.

1　*Know*

(1) recognize; (2) have sexual relations with

2　*Argus*

In classical mythology, a monster
with 100 eyes, employed by the
jealous Hera as a guard for the
imprisoned Io, her husband Zeus's
lover

3　*yet mine own*

Still intact

4　*pen*

Writing utensil (with a play on
"penis")

5　*of credit*

Worthy to be believed (ironic, since
to *Swear by your double self* would be
to swear on the fact that you were
two-faced or double dealing)

I'll not deny him anything I have,

No, not my body, nor my husband's bed.

Know° him I shall, I am well sure of it.

Lie not a night from home. Watch me like Argus.²   230

If you do not, if I be left alone,

Now, by mine honor—which is yet mine own³—

I'll have that doctor for my bedfellow.

Nerissa

[*to* **Gratiano**] And I his clerk. Therefore be well advised

How you do leave me to mine own protection.   235

Gratiano

catch   Well, do you so; let not me take° him then,

For if I do I'll mar the young clerk's pen.⁴

Antonio

I am th' unhappy subject of these quarrels.

Portia

Sir, grieve not you. You are welcome notwithstanding.

Bassanio

Portia, forgive me this enforcèd wrong,   240

And, in the hearing of these many friends,

I swear to thee, even by thine own fair eyes

Wherein I see myself—

Portia

                                    Mark you but that!

In both my eyes he doubly sees himself—

twofold; deceitful   In each eye, one. Swear by your double° self,   245

And there's an oath of credit!⁵

Bassanio

                                          Nay, but hear me.

Pardon this fault, and by my soul I swear

I never more will break an oath with thee.

1   *In lieu of this*

     In exchange for this ring

2   *where the ways are fair enough*

     I.e., when the roads do not need
     to be fixed. Gratiano claims that
     Portia and Nerissa's lesson is un-
     necessary, since he and Bassanio
     were never unfaithful.

3   *cuckolds*

     Husbands whose wives are
     unfaithful

Antonio

prosperity I once did lend my body for his wealth,°

Which but for him that had your husband's ring   250

been destroyed Had quite miscarried.° I dare be bound again,

My soul upon the forfeit, that your lord

intentionally Will never more break faith advisedly.°

Portia

guarantor [*giving* **Antonio** *a ring*] Then you shall be his surety.°

Give him this

And bid him keep it better than the other.   255

Antonio

Here, Lord Bassanio. Swear to keep this ring.

Bassanio

By Heaven, it is the same I gave the doctor!

Portia

from I had it of° him. Pardon me, Bassanio,

For, by this ring, the doctor lay with me.

Nerissa

[*taking out a ring*] And pardon me, my gentle Gratiano,   260

stunted For that same "scrubbèd"° boy, the doctor's clerk,

In lieu of this,¹ last night did lie with me.

Gratiano

Why, this is like the mending of highways

In summer where the ways are fair enough!²

What, are we cuckolds³ ere we have deserved it?   265

Portia

stupidly / confused Speak not so grossly.°—You are all amazed.°

Here is a letter. Read it at your leisure.

It comes from Padua, from Bellario.

There you shall find that Portia was the doctor,

Nerissa there her clerk. Lorenzo here   270

testify Shall witness° I set forth as soon as you,

just And even but° now returned. I have not yet

1   *dumb*

Dumbstruck; at a loss for words

Entered my house.—Antonio, you are welcome.

And I have better news in store for you

Than you expect. [*gives* **Antonio** *a letter*] Unseal this

    letter soon. 275

merchant ships There you shall find three of your argosies°

unexpectedly Are richly come to harbor suddenly.°

You shall not know by what strange accident

I chancèd on this letter.

Antonio

                I am dumb. '

Bassanio

[*to* **Portia**] Were you the doctor, and I knew you not? 280

Gratiano

[*to* **Nerissa**] Were you the clerk that is to make me

    cuckold?

Nerissa

i.e., make you a cuckold Ay, but the clerk that never means to do it,°

Unless he live until he be a man.

Bassanio

[*to* **Portia**] Sweet doctor, you shall be my bedfellow.

When I am absent then lie with my wife. 285

Antonio

livelihood Sweet lady, you have given me life and living.°

For here I read for certain that my ships

harbor Are safely come to road.°

Portia

             How now, Lorenzo?

My clerk hath some good comforts too for you.

Nerissa

Ay, and I'll give them him without a fee. 290

             [*hands* **Lorenzo** *a paper*]

There do I give to you and Jessica,

From the rich Jew, a special deed of gift,

1   *manna*

Divine food, dropped from Heaven
during the Israelites' desert exile
(Exodus 16:15)

2   *satisfied / Of these events at full*

Completely content with my
explanation of what has happened

3   *charge us there upon interr'gatories*

Question us there under oath (as if
in court)

4   *ring*

The play ends with one final pun,
with *ring*, in addition to its obvious
meaning, a slang term for "vagina"

After his death, of all he dies possessed of.

Lorenzo

Fair ladies, you drop manna[1] in the way
Of starvèd people.

Portia

It is almost morning,   295
And yet I am sure you are not satisfied
Of these events at full.[2] Let us go in,
And charge us there upon interr'gatories,[3]
And we will answer all things faithfully.

Gratiano

Let it be so. The first interr'gatory   300
That my Nerissa shall be sworn on is
wait   Whether till the next night she had rather stay°
until   Or go to bed now, being two hours to° day.
            But were the day come, I should wish it dark,
lying   Till I were couching° with the doctor's clerk.   305
            Well, while I live I'll fear no other thing
greatly   So sore° as keeping safe Nerissa's ring.[4]   *They exit.*

The comicall History of the Mer-
chant of Venice.

Enter *Anthonio, Salaryno,* and *Salanio.*

An. IN footh I know not why I am fo fad,
It wearies me, you fay it wearies you;
But how I caught it, found it, or came by it,
What ftuffe tis made of, whereof it is borne,
I am to learne : and fuch a want-wit fadnes
makes of mee,
That I haue much adoe to know my felfe.

Salarino. Your minde is toffing on the Ocean,
There where your Argofies with portlie fayle
Like Signiors and rich Burgars on the flood,
Or as it were the Pageants of the fea,
Doe ouer-peere the petty traffiquers
That curfie to them do them reuerence
As they flie by them with theyr wouen wings.

Salanio. Beleeue mee fir, had I fuch venture forth,
The better part of my affections would
Be with my hopes abroade. I fhould be ftill
Plucking the graffe to know where fits the wind,
Piring in Maps for ports, and peers and rodes :
And euery obiect that might make me feare
Mif-fortune to my ventures, out of doubt
Would make me fad.

Salar. My wind cooling my broth,
vvould blow me to an ague when I thought
vvhat harme a winde too great might doe at fea.
I fhould not fee the fandie howre-glaffe runne
But I fhould thinke of fhallowes and of flatts,
And fee my wealthy *Andrew* docks in fand

A 2.   Vayling

Editing *The Merchant of Venice*
by David Scott Kastan

T he earliest text of *The Merchant of Venice* was the Quarto published in 1600 (Q1), though the play was most likely written in 1597. A second quarto edition (Q2) was published in 1619 with a title page falsely dated 1600, and the play was included among the comedies in the 1623 Folio (F). Both Q2 and F were printed from a copy of the 1600 Quarto, each making a few obvious corrections and each introducing some errors, so Q1 unquestionably provides the most authoritative text of the play. (A "quarto" refers to a book made from sheets of paper each folded twice to provide four leaves or eight pages; a folio is a larger book made from sheets of paper folded once to provide two leaves or four pages.)

The 1600 Quarto seems to have been printed from a manu-script, possibly one in Shakespeare's own hand, but in any case not a perfectly worked out theatrical copy, as a number of indeterminate stage directions (e.g., "*Enter . . . three or four followers*" at the beginning of Act Two) as well as several missing entrances and exits suggest. The manuscript, however, does not seem to have posed any great diffi-culty for the printers. The most serious textual problems posed by the play result primarily from ambiguous and shifting speech prefixes, some of which seem the result of type shortages.

In general, the editorial work of this present edition is conservative, preserving and clarifying the text that appears in Q1, emending only when it is manifestly in error (and recording these changes in the Textual Notes). All other changes to the Quarto text are in accord with modern practices of editing Shakespeare: normalizing spelling, capitalization, and punctuation, removing superfluous italics, regularizing the names of characters, and rationalizing entrances and exits. Editorial stage directions are kept to a minimum and added always in brackets.

A comparison of the edited text of Act One, scene one, lines 1–22 with the facsimile page of the Quarto (on p. 276) reveals many of the issues in this process of editing. Names are regularized, so the names in the Quarto's opening stage direction, *Anthonio*, *Salaryno*, and *Salanio* become here and throughout **Antonio**, **Salarino**, and **Solanio**. The speech prefixes themselves are expanded for clarity, so that *An.* in the first line becomes **Antonio** and *Salar.* at line 22 **Salarino**.

The kind of substantive change that is made to the Quarto can be seen in lines 26–27, where the Quarto reads "I should . . . see my wealthy *Andrew* docks in sand." The text as printed makes no sense, though it appears in both Q and F. Editors have suggested various changes, but "docked" seems the simplest and most likely (based on an easy misreading of the manuscript), and it is what this edition prints.

Normally, however, changes to the Quarto text are matters only of modernization. Spelling throughout is regularized to reflect modern spelling practices. As spelling in Shakespeare's time had not yet been standardized, words were spelled in various ways that indicated their proximate pronunciation, and compositors, in any case, were under no obligation to follow the spelling of their copy. Little, then, is to be gained in an edition such as this by following the spelling of the original printed text. Therefore in line 4 "stuffe" unproblematically becomes "stuff" and "borne" "born"; "sadnes" in line 6 becomes "sadness," and "portlie" in line 9 becomes "portly." As these indicate, old spellings are consistently modernized, but old *forms* of words (e.g., "morrow" for "morning") are retained. The capitalized first letters of many nouns in the Quarto (e.g., "Ocean" in line 8 or "Argosies" in line 9) are reduced to lowercase, except where modern punctuation would demand them. Punctuation, too, is adjusted to reflect modern practice (which is designed to clarify the logical relations between grammatical units, unlike seventeenth-century punctuation, which was dominated by rhythmical concerns), since the punctuation is no more likely than the spelling or capitalization to be Shakespeare's own. Thus, in the Quarto Salarino responds to Antonio's sadness:

> Your mind is tossing on the Ocean,
> There where your Argosies with portlie sayle
> Like Signiors and rich Burgars on the flood,
> Or as it were the Pageants of the sea,
> Doe ouer-peere the petty traffiquers
> That cursie to them do them reuerence
> As they flie by them with theyr wouen wings.

Modernized this reads:

> Your mind is tossing on the ocean,
> There where your argosies with portly sail,
> (Like signiors and rich burghers on the flood
> Or, as it were, the pageants of the sea)
> Do overpeer the petty traffickers
> That curtsy to them, do them reverence
> As they fly by them with their woven wings. (1.1.8–14)

No doubt there is some loss in this modernization. Clarity and consistency is gained at the expense of some loss of expressive detail, but normalizing spelling, capitalization, and punctuation allows the text to be read with far greater ease than the original, and essentially as it was intended to be understood. Seventeenth-century readers would have been unsurprised to find "u" for "v" in "ouer-peer" in line 12 or "reuerence" in line 13 or "wouen" in the next line. Nor would they be confused by the spelling "sayle" in line 9 for "sail" or "theyr" in line 14 for "their." The intrusive "e"s in a word like "Doe" in line 12 would not have seemed odd, nor would the "literary" capitalization of the nouns in the passage. The comma we expect in the middle of line 13 is absent in Q but is unlikely to have misled a reader. Modernizing in all these cases clarifies rather than alters Shakespeare's intentions. If necessarily in modernization we do lose the historical feel of the text Shakespeare's contemporaries read, it is important to note that Shakespeare's contemporaries would not have thought the Quarto in any sense archaic or quaint, as these details inevitably make it for a reader today. The text would have seemed to them as modern as this one does to us. Indeed, many of the Quarto's typographical peculiarities are the result of its effort to make the printed page look up to date for potential buyers.

Modern readers, however, cannot help but be distracted by the different conventions they encounter on the Quarto page. While it is indeed of interest to see how orthography and typography have changed over time, these changes are not primary concerns for most readers of this edition. What little, then, is lost in a careful modernization of the text is more than made up for by the removal of the artificial obstacle of unfamiliar spelling forms and punctuation habits, which neither the playwright nor his publishers could have intended as interpretive difficulties for Shakespeare's readers.

Textual Notes

The list below records all substantive departures in this edition from the text of the 1600 Quarto. It does not record modernizations of

spelling, corrections of obvious typographical errors, standardiza-
tion of capitals, adjustments of lineation, rationalizations of speech
prefixes (SP), and minor repositioning or rewording of stage directions (SD). The adopted reading in this edition is given first in boldface
and followed by the original, rejected reading of Q1, or noted as being
absent from the Quarto text. If the accepted reading appears either in
Q2 or F, that fact is indicated in the collation below in brackets (i.e.,
[Q2] or [F]). Editorial stage directions are not collated but are enclosed
within brackets in the text. Latin stage directions are translated (e.g.,
They exit for *Exeunt*), and act and scene designations, completely absent
from the Quarto, are supplied.

1.1.13 curtsy [F curtsey] cursie; **1.1.19 Peering [F]** Piring; **1.1.27 docked**
docks; **1.1.57 Here** *Sola.* Here; **1.1.98 damn** dam; **1.1.113 Is** It is; **1.1.128
off** of; **1.1.151 back** bake; **1.2.44–45 An you** & you; **1.2.51 le Bon** Le
Boune; **1.2.56 throstle** Trassell; **1.2.61 Falconbridge** Fauconbridge;
1.2.79 vilely vildlie; **1.2.80 vilely** vildly; **1.3.17 Rialto** Ryalta; **1.3.27SP,
30SP, 37SP Shylock** Iew (or Jew)

2.1.0SD Morocco Morochus; **2.1.35 page** rage; **2.2.1SP Launcelot**
Clowne (throughout); **2.2.3 "Gobbo," "Launcelot Gobbo,"** Iobbe,
Launcelet Iobbe [Iobbo is Q's spelling throughout this first speech,
and Launcelet is the spelling throughout.]; **2.2.41 By** Be; **2.2.92 last**
[Q2] lost; **2.2.151 Eleven [Q2]** a leuen; **2.4.8 four o'clock** foure of clock;
2.5.0SD Enter [Shylock] Enter Iewe; **2.5.1SP Shylock** Iewe; **2.5.41 Jewess'** Iewes; **2.6.25 Ho** Howe; **2.6.52 Beshrew** Beshrow; **2.7.0SD Morocco** Morrocho; **2.7.24 Morocco** Morocho; **2.7.69 tombs** timber;
2.7.74 Cold *Mor.* Cold; **2.8.8 gondola** Gondylo; **2.8.39 Slubber [Q2, F]**
Slumber; **2.9.47 chaff [Q2, F]** chaft; **2.9.63 judgment** [Q2] iudement;
2.9.100 Bassanio, Lord Love, Bassanio Lord, loue

3.1.6 Report report; **3.1.18 lest** least; **3.1.26 fledged** [Q2, F] flidge; **3.1.43 court'sy** [Q2, F] cursie; **3.1.65SP Man** [not in Q]; **3.1.84** (2x), **85 o'** a; **3.1.93 Heard** here; **3.1.105 turquoise** Turkies; **3.2.7 lest** least; **3.2.14 Beshrew** Beshrow; **3.2.23 eke** eche; **3.2.63SP** [not in Q]; **3.2.66SP** [not in Q]; **3.2.66 Reply; reply.** [in Q set in italics to the right of line 65]; **3.2.67SP** [not in Q]; **3.2.67 eyes** [F] eye; **3.2.81 vice** voice; **3.2.84 stairs** stayers; **3.2.110 shudd'ring** [F] shyddering; **3.2.117 whether** [F] whither; **3.2.204 roof** [Q2] rough; **3.2.216 an** and; **3.2.242 shrewd** shrowd; **3.2.314SP Bassanio** [not in Q]; **3.3.0SD Shylock** [not in Q]; **3.3.0SD Solanio** [F] Salerio; **3.3.1SP Shylock** Iew [throughout the scene]; **3.3.24SP Solanio** Sal; **3.4.49 Padua** Mantua; **3.4.50 cousin's hand** [F] cosin hands; **3.4.53 traject** Tranect; **3.4.81 my** [Q2, F] my my; **3.5.4 o'** a; **3.5.19 e'en** [Q2, F] in; **3.5.24 comes** [Q2, F] come; **3.5.49 show** shewe; **3.5.69 merit it** meane it, it; **3.5.76 a** [F] [not in Q]; **3.5.81 howsome'er** how so mere

4.1.30 his state [Q2, F] this states; **4.1.31 flint** [Q2] flints; **4.1.35SP Shylock** Iewe [through l. 174]; **4.1.51 Masters oft** Maisters of; **4.1.74 bleat** [F] bleake; **4.1.75 mountain** [F] mountaine of; **4.1.100 'Tis** [Q2, F] as; **4.1.228 No** Not; **4.1.233 tenor** [Q2] tenure; **4.1.248SP Shylock** Iew [through l. 302]; **4.1.256 lest** least; **4.1.316SP Shylock** Iew; **4.1.396SP Gratiano** Shy; **4.2.11 show** shew

5.1.21 shrew shrow; **5.1.26SP Stephano.** Mess. [throughout scene]; **5.1.41 Master Lorenzo?** Lorenzo, & M.; **5.1.47–48 ere morning.** ere morning sweete soule.; **5.1.49 Sweet soul, let's** Let's; **5.1.51 Stephano** [Q2] Stephen; **5.1.87 Erebus** [F Erobus] Terebus; **5.1.152 give it** [Q2, F] giue; **5.1.233 my** [Q2, F] mine

The Merchant of Venice on the Early Stage
by Julie Crawford

O n the title page of its first published edition, even before we are told that it was "Written by William Shakespeare," *The Merchant of Venice* is identified as having "been diverse times acted by the Lord Chamberlain and his servants." This was clearly one of the play's selling points; the Lord Chamberlain's Men were among the most popular actors in Elizabethan England. Shakespeare himself was a chief shareholder in the company, and his investment in the success of his play was undoubtedly as commercial as it was artistic. In 1596–1597, when the play was first performed, the Lord Chamberlain's Men were performing at smaller theaters before moving to the Globe, the larger suburban outdoor theater, in 1599. Yet the first recorded performances of *The Merchant of Venice* were at James I's court during the Shrove holiday of 1605. From the beginning of its stage history, *The Merchant of Venice* was clearly performed for a wide variety of audiences.

A now lost play called *The Jew*, also about usury, had been performed in 1578, and, more recently, Christopher Marlowe's *The Jew of Malta* (written around 1589) had been a continuing success for a rival company. The allusions to and competition with Marlowe's play are both implicit and explicit in Shakespeare's. When Shylock refers to "Barabbas" (4.1.294), the audience would have thought not only of

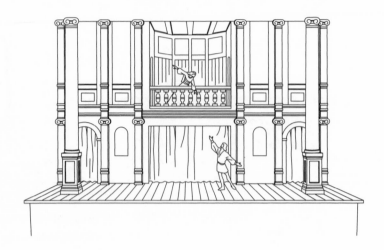

Fig 1. *In the large London playhouses, the balcony above the stage could be used for staging, seating, or to house musicians.*

Fig 2. *English Renaissance drama made minimal use of sets or backdrops. In the absence of a set, the stage pillars could be incorporated into the action, standing in for trees and other architectural elements.*

Fig 3. The discovery space, located in the middle of the backstage wall, could be used as a third entrance as well as a location for scenes requiring special staging, such as in a tomb or bedchamber.

Fig 4. A trapdoor led to the area below the stage, known as "Hell" (as contrasted with the painted ceiling, known as "Heaven" or the "heavens"). Ghosts or other supernatural figures could descend through the trap, and it could also serve as a grave.

the murderer whom the Jews freed instead of Christ but also of the diabolical and popular main character in Marlowe's play. Long before Marlowe, there was a powerful theatrical history of caricatured Jews on the stage, and, as the play makes clear by its nine comparisons between devils and Jews, Shakespeare's presentation of Shylock owed a great deal to medieval morality plays. In addition to frequently presenting Jews as embodiments of evil, morality plays also featured an Everyman figure who is tempted by Vice characters and the Devil. Launcelot Gobbo's conscience-wrestling about whether he should work for Shylock or Bassanio is partly a parody of the decision Everyman makes about whether to serve God or the Devil; the Jew, Launcelot claims, "is a kind of devil" (2.2.22). While it is clear that Shylock is far more than an allegory, everyone watching Shakespeare's play would have recognized its anti-Jewish theatrical history.

The Merchant of Venice is also firmly set Venice, a setting that would have had specific connotations for early modern theatergoers as a place where the trade and profit "Consisteth of all nations" (3.3.31). The play alternates scenes between Venice and Belmont (we learn when the disguised Portia and Nerissa leave Belmont for Venice that the two locations are not very far apart), but there were not different sets for the two locations. Indeed there were almost no sets at all for any early modern play, just the five-foot-high stage with its supporting pillars and two entrances at the back and a recessed discovery place, often with a balcony above it, between them. Instead locations were evoked by description, the characters who inhabit them (merchants or aristocrats), the type of language spoken there, the kinds of activities that occupy the characters' time (hazardous borrowing or hazardous wooing), and props. Shylock frequently refers to the Rialto, the commercial center of Venice, locating us not only in a place but in a set of values. We are also told at one point that Lorenzo and Jessica were seen in a gondola, an iconic Venetian detail.

Props were few on the Shakespearean stage, but the ones that did appear were powerfully symbolic. When Portia "draw[s] aside the curtains and discover[s] / The several caskets" (2.7.1–2), we are reminded of the earlier scene in which Jessica throws one of her father's caskets out the window to a waiting Lorenzo—"Here, catch this casket" (2.6.33). In all likelihood, the casket Jessica throws is one of the caskets that Portia reveals behind the curtain. The fact that these two scenes use the same prop and take place in the same location on the stage, the discovery place, encourages the audience to think about the differences between the two daughters' relationships to their fathers' wills and property, and between their romantic and marital options. The added detail of the balcony (as Gratiano says, "This is the penthouse under which Lorenzo / Desired us to make stand" [2.6.1–2]), already famous from plays like *Romeo and Juliet* (1594–1595) as the location of secretive love and seduction, highlights both Jessica's willfulness and her betrayal of her father's commands to lock his house and not to "thrust [her] head into the public street / To gaze on Christian fools" (2.5.31–32). The spareness of the early modern stage was thus less a limitation than an opportunity to highlight the contrasts and similarities between different settings, characters, and objects of exchange.

If the Shakespearean stage had limited settings—we only know that the entirety of Act Five takes place at night because the characters keep telling us so—it had excellent costumes. When Launcelot leaves Shylock to work for Bassanio, whom, he tells us, "gives rare new liveries [uniforms]" (2.2.102–103) to his servants, and Bassanio in turn commands that Launcelot be given a particularly fancy uniform, the actor playing Launcelot may well have reappeared wearing a livery that actually came from one of the aristocratic families of England. (There was a brisk market in secondhand clothes surrounding the early modern theater.) Evocative of key themes in the play—the proverbial truth that "The world is still deceived with ornament"

(3.2.74)—Launcelot's probable costume change also reminded early modern audiences of the fact that clothes did, in many ways, make the man. Shylock's much-discussed "Jewish gaberdine," or long coat (1.3.108), works in a similarly resonant way. One of his few physically identifying characteristics (a detail suggesting that Shylock was not meant to be a physical caricature), Shylock himself draws attention to his dress by a description of Antonio spitting on it, a vivid emblem of otherness and its humiliations. At other, rarer, points, the play script itself offers explicit stage directions about the way a character is supposed to look: All of the early published editions of the play tell us that the prince of Morocco is "a tawny Moor all in white" (2.1.0.1), suggesting visual difference both at the level of skin color and dress ("Moor" could refer to both Muslim religion or complexion). Portia's references to the prince of Morocco's "complexion" have a number of connotations, but makeup was undoubtedly used to indicate representative rather than realistic difference. In contrast, it has been suggested that when Shylock says to the Venetians, "You have among you many a purchased slave" (4.1.90), he may have gestured toward actual Africans playing Venetian servants, as they would have been present not only in Venice but also in Shakespeare's England. The prince of Morocco himself mentions his "scimitar"—a decidedly Eastern stage prop—but makes it clear that it has been used to kill fellow Muslims (the Sophy and a Persian prince) rather than Christians. The later embedded stage direction, Bassanio's questioning of Shylock, "Why dost thou whet [sharpen] thy knife so earnestly?" (4.1.121), thus both reminds us of the play's concern with the threat of knives in the hands of others and literalizes the bloodthirstiness of Shylock's bond as something chillingly close to home.

Like costume, cross-dressing plays an important role in *The Merchant of Venice*. Women's parts were played by boy actors on the early modern stage—women acted in other venues in the early modern period—but we also see no fewer than three women characters cross-dressing in the course of the play. Jessica dresses as a page to escape her father's house and Portia and Nerissa as a doctor and a clerk to save Antonio's life. While Jessica regards her cross-dressing with shame ("Cupid himself would blush / To see me thus transformèd to a boy" [2.6.38–39]), Portia and Nerissa have a lot more fun with theirs. Portia mocks male fantasies about women (particularly their "quaint lies" about their success with the ladies [3.4.69]) and jokes about wearing a dagger and showing her "whole device" to Nerissa in the privacy of her coach (3.4.81). But she also jokes about speaking "between the change of man and boy" (3.4.66), alluding to the boy actor beneath the clothes, a boy whose voice might well be changing. Similarly, when Portia and Nerissa are reconciling with their husbands, there is a great deal of play on the multiple erotic possibilities of cross-dressed characters. Bassanio's joke near the end of the play, "Sweet doctor, you shall be my bedfellow" (5.1.284), relies on the audience's knowledge that there was a boy actor beneath the doctor's clothes as well as a woman. While some feared the erotic suggestiveness of the transvestite theater, others clearly enjoyed it, and, in *The Merchant of Venice*, the homoerotic suggestiveness of these scenes further highlights the complex nature of Antonio and Bassanio's relationship.

It might be helpful to think of the play in your hands as a script to be filled in—and abbreviated—by the actors performing it. (If we performed the full text of *The Merchant of Venice* it would take us over three hours; the early modern players had only two hours use of the stage to work with.) While there is no hard evidence, most scholars believe that the famous comic actor Will Kemp played Launcelot. (If true, this detail would add an interesting gloss to the character's claim that he has grown "famished" [2.2.99] and rib-exposed in his service to Shylock; Kemp was famously muscular.) Indeed, if many in the audience came to see a play about a merchant and a Jew, they also came to see the actors, especially the comic ones. When Lorenzo says to Launcelot, "Wilt thou show the whole wealth of thy wit in an instant?" (3.5.49–50), he was alluding on some level to the notorious ad-libbing of Shakespeare stage clowns; Hamlet insists that in his play the "clowns speak no more than is set down for them" (3.2.37). Each performance, whether for the underlings at the Globe or for the dignitaries of the court, was in many ways a unique event, created not only by Shakespeare but also by the actors and the audience who solicited and responded to their efforts.

Significant Performances
by Julie Crawford

1598 On July 22, 1598, the play is registered for publication with the Stationers' Company, suggesting that it had been in performance for some time.

1600 The title page of the first published edition of the play states that it has "been diverse times acted by the Lord Chamberlain and his servants," Shakespeare's company.

1605 The earliest stage performances were during the Shrove holiday at the Court of James I on February 10 and 12, 1605.

1701 George Granville, Lord Lansdowne staged a successful adaptation entitled *The Jew of Venice*, which reduced the number of scenes from twenty to nine and sought to play up the play's "Manly and Moral Graces." In particular, the play featured Bassanio—performed by a sixty-six-year-old—as the romantic hero. This version was performed for the next forty years.

1741 Instead of playing Shylock as a comic figure, the Irish-born actor, dramatist, and bad boy Charles Macklin prepared for his role by researching Italian Jews. He debuted on February 14, 1741, at the

Theatre Royal in Drury Lane in a production that returned to Shakespeare's original text. Macklin's Shylock made him the most famous actor of his time, and he performed the role for almost fifty years.

1814 From the opening performance in Drury Lane on January 26, 1814, Edmund Kean's Shylock was an immediate sensation. As the well-known essayist and drama critic William Hazlitt put it, Kean's Shylock was "a man more sinned against than sinning." In many ways, Kean's performance inaugurated the tradition of portraying Shylock sympathetically. During the production's run, Act Five was often omitted, and the play ended with Shylock's departure.

1879 Actor-manager Henry Irving mounted a production of the play at the Lyceum Theatre in 1879. Featuring elaborate sets (including a useable bridge), and the famed actress Ellen Terry as a (nonetheless censored) Portia, the play was most famous for Irving's portrayal of Shylock as what one observer called "the only gentleman in the play, and most ill-used." The great playwright and critic George Bernard Shaw was less enthusiastic about Irving's interpretation, remarking that his "huge and enduring success as Shylock was due to his absolutely refusing to allow Shylock to be the discomforted villain of the piece. *The Merchant of Venice* became 'The Martyrdom of Irving,' which was, it must be confessed, far finer than 'The Tricking of Shylock.'" Despite Shaw's criticism, Irving's production became the most influential version ever produced, running for 250 performances during its first season and, over the course of twenty-five years, for one thousand performances in England and America.

1901 The first important Yiddish production, with the Russian refugee Jacob Adler as Shylock, was presented in 1901 at the People's Theater in the Bowery section of Manhattan. In 1903, Adler performed

Shylock on Broadway, speaking Yiddish while the rest of the cast spoke English.

1914   A silent-movie version of the play was directed by Lois Weber. Weber, who also stars as Portia, was the first woman to direct a full-length feature film.

1930s   During the 1930s, the play was revived as a kind of challenge to the rise of Nazism and the deprivation of Jewish rights. It was produced in Yiddish in Warsaw and in Hebrew in Tel Aviv, in both cases by German Jewish directors who had become refugees from their homeland.

1943   The play has had a long history of performance in Germany and Austria, but one of the most famous productions premiered on May 15, 1943, at the Vienna Burgtheater, and it has been singled out as the most infamous incidence of theater's complicity with the Nazi regime.

1947   An attempt to produce the play in Frankfurt in 1947 was vigorously opposed, and the chairman of the municipal theater had to resign. The same year, the Shubert Organization in New York requested that the visiting Donald Wolfit Shakespeare Company, scheduled to appear in a Shubert-controlled house, eliminate the play from its New York repertory because of its offensiveness to Jews.

1962   When Joseph Papp produced the play in Central Park with George C. Scott as Shylock, many of the city's top rabbis protested. Rabbi Louis I. Newman declared in his sermon at Congregation Rodeph Sholom that "for the city to give its auspices to a play that has created injury and is hate-provoking is obnoxious." When their efforts failed, the rabbis sought to curtail CBS's telecast of the production. CBS eventually submitted, broadcasting only on local New York stations.

1981   When PBS announced plans to broadcast the BBC's production of *The Merchant of Venice*, the Anti-Defamation League sought an injunction to prevent the transmission on the grounds that the play might incite racial hatred against Jewish Americans.

1987   In Bill Alexander's production for the Royal Shakespeare Company, a lynch mob hurtled through the streets of Venice spraying swastikas on walls and chanting anti-Jewish slogans. According to some critics, the actor playing Shylock, the South African Jew Anthony Sher, who performed the role in flowing robes and a turban, seemed almost to invite controversy.

2002   A New Zealand company produced the Maori *The Merchant of Venice* based on a 1945 translation of the play into Maori by Dr. Pei Te Hurinui Jones.

2004   The film adaptation directed by Michael Radford stars Al Pacino as Shylock, Jeremy Irons as Antonio, Joseph Fiennes as Bassanio, and Lynn Collins as Portia.

2007   Another film version, written by John Logan and starring Sir Ian McKellen and Patrick Stewart, is set in a Las Vegas casino.

See the Shakespeare in Production series, *The Merchant of Venice*, edited by Charles Edelman (Cambridge: Cambridge Univ. Press, 2002).

Inspired by *The Merchant of Venice*

T he *Merchant of Venice* is one of Shakespeare's most frequently performed plays. Several key phrases from
the text have filtered into our common vocabulary,
including "The quality of mercy is not strained"
and "All that glisters is not gold" (although Shakespeare's *glisters* is usually rendered as "glitters").
However, *Merchant* remains a deeply troubling play to many, mostly
due to its complicated villain, Shylock, and the ambiguous stance
Shakespeare seems to take toward his creation. Is Shylock a bad man
who happens to be Jewish or is he bad *because* he is Jewish? Alternatively we might ask, is *The Merchant of Venice* an anti-Semitic play? Or is
it simply a play that engages with anti-Semitic stereotypes without
necessarily endorsing them? The tension that lies at the heart of
Merchant makes it an uncomfortable experience for many readers and
audience members, but it is also the quality that has allowed the play
to have such a rich and diverse cultural legacy, as generations of artists have sought their own answers to the play's central mysteries.

Stage

In 1656, Oliver Cromwell, the Lord Protector of Great Britain, repealed
a medieval statute expelling Jews from England. Jews—some of who

were already living in England as *conversos*, or Christian converts, while continuing to practice their faith in secret—were allowed to resettle in England and openly establish a synagogue. The earliest extant adaptation of *The Merchant of Venice*, George Granville's *The Jew of Venice* (c. 1701), may have been inspired by these events and the increased Jewish presence in England in the seventeenth century. Like many early adaptations of Shakespeare's plays, *The Jew of Venice* is a revised version of Shakespeare's text, with certain characters omitted and scenes rewritten. Gobbo and his father, Shylock's friend Tubal, and the princes of Morocco and Aragon are among the dropped characters. Granville also added material, including an extended banquet scene that featured a masque, or musical performance, entitled Peleus and Thetis. The courtroom scene takes on a melodramatic feel, as Bassanio offers to sacrifice himself for his friend Antonio and then threatens the judge with his sword.

In the nineteenth century, theatrical productions that parodied well-known stories and characters became highly popular. Shakespeare's plays were frequent targets of these satirical Victorian performances, known as burlesques. There were at least two such versions of *The Merchant of Venice*: Francis Talfourd's *Shylock or, the Merchant of Venice Preserved* (1849) and the Christy's Minstrels' *Shylock* (c. 1870). In accordance with the conventions of the genre, both plays employed puns, songs, and topical allusions to send up more serious-minded productions of the original Shakespearean text. Actors playing Shylock, for instance, usually wore fake noses and red beards to comically portray the character as a stereotypical Jew. The up-and-coming comedian Frederick Robson played Shylock in Talfourd's production, billed as a "Jerusalem Hearty-Joke." While both burlesques portrayed Shylock as a buffoon, Robson's performance was noted for also emphasizing Shylock's tragic side.

In the latter half of the twentieth century, adaptations of Shakespeare's play began to actively engage questions about the political ramifications of World War II as well as the cultural legacy of anti-Semitism. Charles Marowitz's 1976 *Variations on the Merchant of Venice*, which liberally incorporates and rearranges Shakespeare's dialogue, presents a highly politicized reading of *The Merchant of Venice*. The play is set in Jerusalem in 1946, when limits the British had placed on Jewish immigration into British Palestine made them the object of frequent terrorist attacks. Marowitz makes the Venetian characters British and Shylock, although still a moneylender, a supporter of covert terrorist activities, such as the bombing that opens the play. This play continues the tradition of presenting Shylock as a character whose morals are difficult to interpret: as both freedom fighter and terrorist, it is unclear whether Shylock deserves the audience's sympathy, condemnation, or both.

The playwright Arnold Wesker complained that the anti-Semitism of *The Merchant of Venice* was embedded in the text itself, and that no performance could redeem it. As a result, in 1977 he wrote *The Merchant* as a truly sympathetic portrayal of the Jewish protagonist. *The Merchant* portrays Shylock as a loan banker who is good friends with Antonio. Shylock wants to loan Antonio the money without a bond, but Venetian law prevents him from doing so. The play develops into a conflict between Shylock's loyalty to the Jewish community and his personal loyalty to his friend. In the end, he chooses to commit suicide rather than destroy Antonio.

A. R. Gurney's 1996 *Overtime* bills itself as a "modern sequel" to *The Merchant of Venice*. Gurney's play takes place immediately after Shakespeare's ends, with Portia throwing a party to celebrate her success in court as well as her upcoming marriage to Bassanio. Although ostensibly set in the same time period as *Merchant*, the absurdist comedy plays fast and loose with historical accuracy. Gurney turns Shakespeare's characters into a thoroughly modern, multicultural lot: Portia becomes a country-clubbing WASP; Bassanio, a Bostonian Irish American obsessed with sports and beer; and Jessica becomes a "Jewish American princess." Nerissa and Gratiano are depicted as a Latina and an African American man who begin to resent their second-class status in Venice and start aggressively asserting their ethnic identities. As the tensions between the various characters threatens to disrupt the party—and Portia's idealistic vision of a more open-minded, diverse "new Venice" starts to unravel—the charismatic, sympathetic Shylock arrives to help set things right.

Shylock, a one-man play written and performed by Welsh actor Gareth Armstrong, has toured internationally since its premiere in 1997. In it, Armstrong plays Tubal, Shylock's friend and fellow money-lender who also happens to be "the only other Jewish man in the whole of Shakespeare." Over the course of the eighty-minute performance, Tubal offers both a history lesson and an exploration of his friend's character and legacy. He performs several scenes from *The Merchant of Venice* and holds forth on a number of topics, including the theatrical history of the title character, the political issues involved in performing Shakespeare's play today, and atrocities committed against Jews dating as far back as A.D. 1190.

Visual Art

The popularity of *The Merchant of Venice* in the eighteenth and nineteenth centuries led many artists of the period to depict the play in their artworks. The German-born artist Johan Zoffany based a series of paintings on a 1768–1769 performance of *Merchant* at Covent Garden, in which the famous actor Charles Macklin starred as Shylock. Known for resisting the comedic interpretations of Shylock that had dominated the British stage till that point, Macklin played Shylock for nearly fifty years. One portrait in this series shows Macklin as a sympathetic and frustrated Shylock with his hands stretched out, fists clenched, and a pleading expression on his face. Another painting in the series depicts a dramatic moment in the trial scene: Antonio's shirt is open, exposing his chest, and Shylock holds a knife ready to extract his pound of flesh. Renderings of famous Shakespearean actors in character continued to be a popular genre on through the early twentieth century: in 1886 Sir John Everett Millais painted actress Kate Dolan as Portia in the trial scene, and in 1914 Charles Buchel painted actor Sir Herbert Beerbohm Tree as Shylock.

Paintings that depicted specific moments from *The Merchant of Venice* were also common throughout the eighteenth and nineteenth centuries. In 1795, Richard Westall painted *Shylock Rebuffing Antonio*, a depiction of the moment in Act Three, scene three when Shylock refuses Antonio's offer to repay the bond. In 1835, Thomas Sully painted *Portia and Shylock*, which illustrates Portia's lines to Shylock, "Be merciful. / Take thrice thy money. Bid me tear the bond" (4.1.231–232). Sully makes no attempt to depict Portia in men's clothing but instead paints her with pale skin, feminine features, and long curly hair. British artist Sir John Gilbert was a particularly prolific Shakespeare illustrator, providing artwork for eighteen different print editions of the plays in the nineteenth century. For Charles Knight's edition of Shakespeare's works, Gilbert made a steel-cut engraving titled *Shylock After the Trial*, which shows Shylock in a rage, his arms raised high and a cane in one hand, as he runs from a mob of children. The engraving depicts an imagined scene, however, as Shylock does not actually appear on stage again after the trial in Shakespeare's play.

Depictions of Shylock and his daughter Jessica, or else Jessica alone, were equally popular during the period. Although modern audiences often relegate the Jessica/Lorenzo love story to the periphery of *The Merchant of Venice*, the frequent representations of Jessica suggest a keen interest in this romantic subplot. Robert Smirke's *The Merchant of Venice* (1795), Gilbert Stuart Newton's *Shylock and Jessica from "The Merchant of Venice"* (1830), and Maurycy Gottlieb's *Shylock and Jessica* (1876) all depict a demure, obedient Jessica watched over by a stern Shylock. In each instance, however, Jessica is either clutching or receiving the keys to Shylock's house, reminding the viewer of her imminent escape and elopement with Lorenzo. Likewise, solo por-traits of Jessica emphasize the heroine's connection to the world beyond her father's control. Joseph Mallord William Turner's *Jessica* (1830) portrays Shylock's daughter throwing open the windows and boldly looking out toward the viewer. In William Quiller Orchardson's *Jessica* (1877), the artist clearly displays the keys hanging from Jessica's dress as she cautiously draws back the drapes of the room. Samuel Luke Fields renders his *Jessica* (1888) demurely gazing down from a bal-cony, presumably to the street below.

Novels and Short Stories

Twentieth-century fiction that invokes *The Merchant of Venice* tends to concern itself with William Shakespeare the artist, as well as the pos-sible biographical sources for his play. For example, Anthony Burgess's 1969 short story "The Muse" tells of a Shakespearean scholar, Paley, who travels to a parallel-universe version of Elizabethan England. The Shakespeare he meets there is a shape-shifting monster and a hack to boot, a fraud who steals manuscripts from scholars like Paley and passes them off as his own. The text Shakespeare takes from Paley, which Paley has brought with him from the future, is *The Merchant of Venice*.

Erica Jong mines similar territory in her 1987 novel *Shylock's Daughter* (formerly titled *Serenissima*, a nickname for Venice meaning "the most serene"). Jessica Pruitt is an aging actress who has come to Venice to star in a film version of *Merchant*. One day she meets an old woman in the city's Jewish quarter and, using a ring that the old woman gives her, travels back in time to the sixteenth century, where she finds herself daughter to a Jewish merchant named Shalach. She also meets a young William Shakespeare, and the two embark on a passionate affair. Jong depicts in lurid detail Will's sexual encounters with Jessica in addition to those with several other partners, includ-ing his patron, the Earl of Southampton (long speculated to be the subject of Shakespeare's besotted sonnets). Jessica and Will are eventually forced to flee Venice with Will's infant daughter—whose mother was a young nun named Juliet—but Shalach captures her and brings her back to the city. The sixteenth-century Jessica dies and awakens in the twentieth century with an idea for a new screenplay based on her adventures, just as Shakespeare is inspired to write a play about, in part, a beautiful Jewish girl from Venice.

The idea that a woman inspired Shakespeare to write *The Merchant of Venice* returns in the historical thriller *The Quality of Mercy* (1989) by the well-known mystery writer Faye Kellerman. The novel is inspired by a real-life figure: Roderigo Lopez, the physician to Queen Elizabeth who was accused of and eventually executed for attempting to poison her. The heroine of Kellerman's novel is Roderigo's daughter Rebecca, who, like her father, is a *converso*, or converted Jew. The Lopezes, however, secretly practice their original faith and are committed to helping fellow Jews escape the Spanish Inquisition. Rebecca meets William Shakespeare while both are seeking vengeance for the wrongful death of a loved one, and the two eventually fall in love. Their relationship prompts Shakespeare to write *The Merchant of Venice*, a play sympathetic to the idea of cross-cultural marriage.

For Further Reading
by Julie Crawford

Auden, W. H. "Brothers and Others." *The Dyers Hand* (1963), reprinted in *Shakespeare, The Merchant of Venice: A Casebook.* John Wilders, ed. (Macmillan, 1969). In this groundbreaking essay, Auden highlights both the laws of usury that divided "brothers and others" in the early modern period and the homoerotic complexities of the relationship between Bassanio and Antonio.

Barber, C. L. *Shakespeare's Festive Comedy: A Study of Dramatic Form and Relation to Social Custom* (Princeton University Press, 1959). Barber argues that the play dramatizes the conflict between the mechanisms of wealth and the masterful, social use of it; the festive release of the fifth act can only happen after Shylock is foiled.

Brown, John Russell, ed. *The Merchant of Venice* (Arden; Harvard University Press, 1959). Brown's still frequently cited edition includes excellent appendices of the source texts. His introduction, which includes comprehensive information about the play's early print history, argues that the play represents a battle between love's wealth and crass materialism.

Burckhardt, Sigurd. "*The Merchant of Venice*: The Gentle Bond." *Journal of English Literary History* 29 (1962); reprinted in Shakespeare, *The*

Merchant of Venice: A Casebook. John Wilders, ed. (Macmillan, 1969). Burckhardt argues that the play's plot is circular, bound in such a way that the instrument of destruction, the bond, turns out to be the source of deliverance.

Cohen, Walter. "*The Merchant of Venice* and the Possibilities of Historical Criticism." *English Literary History* 49 (1982): 45–72; reprinted *New Casebooks: The Merchant of Venice*, Martin Coyle, ed. (St. Martin's, 1998). Cohen sees the play's theme as the struggle "between Jewish quasi-feudal fiscalism and native bourgeois mercantilism," and its form as an idealizing resolution of material contradictions that are irreconcilable in reality.

Danson, Lawrence. *The Harmonies of The Merchant of Venice* (Yale University Press, 1978). Danson argues that the play dramatizes the transformation of conflicts into harmonies.

Dessen, Alan C. "The Elizabethan Stage Jew and Christian Example: Gerontus, Barabas, and Shylock." *Modern Language Quarterly* 35 (1974): 231–245. Dessen shows that there was an Elizabethan theatrical tradition in which a stage Jew functions to reveal Christian hypocrisy.

Engle, Lars. "'Thrift is Blessing': Exchange and Explanation in *The Merchant of Venice*." *Shakespeare Quarterly* 37.1 (1986): 20–37. Engle argues that the play is centrally concerned with marriage and credit in an emerging modern economy and that its patterns of credit and debit and payment and profit reveal Portia as the "better manipulator of exchange patterns, and a better idealiser of them" (37).

Halio, Jay L., ed. *The Merchant of Venice* (Oxford University Press, 1993). Halio's introduction provides the most sustained consideration of Shylock and the culture that surrounded both Jewishness and usury.

Hall, Kim F. "Guess Who's Coming to Dinner? Colonization and Miscegenation in *The Merchant of Venice*." *Renaissance Drama* 23 (1992): 87–106. Hall focuses on the silent figure of the female Moor impregnated by Launcelot Gobbo as a way to draw our attention to the imperial- and mercantilist-inspired anxieties over gender, race, and religion that surround the specter of miscegenation in the play.

Lewalski, Barbara. "Biblical Allusion and Allegory in *The Merchant of Venice*." *Shakespeare Quarterly* 13 (1962): 317–343. Lewalski looks at the ways in which the play functions as a battle between the Old Law (Judaism; Law/Justice; Shylock) and the New (Christianity; Love/ Mercy; Antonio/Portia).

Marcus, Leah, ed. *The Merchant of Venice* (Norton, 2005). Marcus's critical edition includes a good range of primary texts, including sixteenth-century texts on usury and Venice, and secondary criticism.

Newman, Karen. "Portia's Ring: Unruly Women and Structures of Exchange in *The Merchant of Venice*." *Shakespeare Quarterly* 38 (1987): 19–33, reprinted in *New Casebooks: The Merchant of Venice*, Martin Coyle, ed. (St. Martin's, 1998). Newman argues that the exchange of goods or women characterizes the play's action in both Venice and Belmont, but that Portia's use of the ring exposes the male homosocial bond that the exchange of women ensures and disrupts the structures of exchange that ensure male power.

Patterson, Steve. "The Bankruptcy of Homoerotic Amity in Shakespeare's *The Merchant of Venice*." *Shakespeare Quarterly* 50.1 (1999): 9–32. Following a long line of critics (see Auden above), Patterson argues that the play queries the advantages of a marriage-based economy over one grounded on amorous male friendships.

Rea, J. D. "Shylock and the Processus Belial." *Philological Quarterly* 8 (1929): 311. Rea points to the similarities between the trial scene and the medieval Processus Belial in which the Devil sues for man's soul on the grounds of justice and the Virgin Mary intervenes on the side of mercy.

Shapiro, James. *Shakespeare and the Jews* (Columbia University Press, 1996). Shapiro argues, among other things, that aspects of the play touch upon ritual Jewish practices like circumcision, and that Shylock's baptism erases the literal and figurative boundaries that distinguish merchant from Jew.